MONASTIC WISDOM

Michael Casey, ocso

The Art of Winning Souls
Pastoral Care of Novices

MONASTIC WISDOM SERIES

Simeon Leiva, ocso, General Editor

Advisory Board

Michael Casey, ocso
Lawrence S. Cunningham
Patrick Hart, ocso
Robert Heller

Terrence Kardong, osb
Kathleen Norris
Miriam Pollard, ocso
Bonnie Thurston

MONASTIC WISDOM SERIES: NUMBER THIRTY-FIVE

The Art of Winning Souls

Pastoral Care of Novices

Michael Casey, ocso

Cistercian Publications
www.cistercianpublications.org

LITURGICAL PRESS
Collegeville, Minnesota
www.litpress.org

A Cistercian Publications title published by Liturgical Press

Cistercian Publications
Editorial Offices
Abbey of Gethsemani
3642 Monks Road
Trappist, Kentucky 40051
www.cistercianpublications.org

Imprimi potest. Abbot David G. Tomlins OCSO
26 November 2010

All translations from Scripture, the Rule of Benedict, the Code of Canon Law, and non-English works are the author's own unless otherwise noted.

© 2012 by Order of Saint Benedict, Collegeville, Minnesota. All rights reserved. No part of this book may be reproduced in any form, by print, microfilm, microfiche, mechanical recording, photocopying, translation, or by any other means, known or yet unknown, for any purpose except brief quotations in reviews, without the previous written permission of Liturgical Press, Saint John's Abbey, P.O. Box 7500, Collegeville, Minnesota 56321-7500. Printed in the United States of America.

2   3   4   5   6   7   8   9

Library of Congress Cataloging-in-Publication Data

Casey, Michael, 1942–
   The art of winning souls : pastoral care of novices / by Michael Casey.
      p. cm. — (Monastic wisdom series ; no. 35)
   Includes bibliographical references (p.   ).
   ISBN 978-0-87907-035-9 — ISBN 978-0-87907-475-3 (e-book)
 1. Spiritual direction. 2. Monastic and religious life. I. Title.
BX2438.C37 2012
255'.12—dc23
                                                                 2012002149

CONTENTS

List of Abbreviations   vii

Introduction   ix

1. Stirring the Possum   1

2. The Work of the Holy Spirit   17
    The School of Christ   21

3. The Community's Work   25
    Transmission of the Charism   28
    Training in the Way of Life   31
    Monastic Education   35

4. A Skilled Senior   40
    Formation of Formators   47

5. Today's Generation   52
    The New Generations   55
    Spirituality   58
    Areas Needing Special Attention   61

6. Assessment of Candidates   77
    Attraction   79
    Assessment   85
    Particular Points   87
    Accepting the Unacceptable   104

7. Building Trust   110

8. The Formative Conversation   135

9. Teaching the Tradition   149
    Adult Learners   149
    Monastic Theology   153
    Reading Texts   158
    Forming a Canon?   161

10. Criteria for Continuance   164
    Suitability   165
    Readiness   172

11. Never Lose Heart   180

Bibliography   185

ABBREVIATIONS

CCCM	*Corpus Christianorum Continuatio Mediævalis* (Turnhout: Brepols)
CChr	*Corpus Christianorum Series Latina* (Turnhout: Brepols)
COCR	*Collectanea Ordinis Cisterciensium Reformatorum* (later *Collectanea Cisterciensia*)
PL	*Patrologia Latina*, ed. J. P. Migne (Turnhout: Brepols)
RB	Rule of Saint Benedict
SBO	*Sancti Bernardi Opera* (Rome: Editiones Cistercienses, 1957–1977)
Div	*De diversis* (*Miscellaneous Sermons*)
JB	Sermon for John the Baptist
PP	Sermon for Peter and Paul
QH	Sermons on Psalm 90
SChr	*Sources Chrétiennes* (Paris: Cerf)

INTRODUCTION

In his chapter on the procedure for the reception of new brothers, Saint Benedict makes provision for entrusting them to the care of "a senior who is skilled in winning souls who will diligently pay attention to them in everything" (RB 58.6). Exactly what this involved in Saint Benedict's time can be discussed from the point of view of history and previous monastic literature. In this book I would like to reflect on what it means today, as I have learned this from my own relatively narrow experience, especially from the mistakes that I have made, and from my exposure to the fruitful ministry of others.

The term "monastic formation" does not mean the same to everyone, either at an intellectual or at an emotional level. If I continue to use it, it is for the sake of convenience, but I understand it in the sense indicated by my subtitle: the pastoral care given in the name of a monastic community to those who enter it, from initial contact up to the point where their vocation has recognizably stabilized. The term "formator" is used of those designated by canon law who have immediate responsibility for initial formation: vocation directors, novice directors, and junior directors—whether these be one, two, or three persons.

These reflections are not intended to be prescriptive. They are, rather, descriptive of what I consider to be best practice, as I have encountered this in my experience of many different expressions of the monastic and Benedictine charism. Inevitably, there will be occasional excursions into what seems to me bad practice—in the sense that it is sometimes instructive to review approaches that do not provide for the long-term sustainability of the attraction to monastic life. These are such that they allow those who enter to avoid the specific challenges of the early years with the result that those who come never lay down foundations strong enough to support a monastic future.

I have taken the liberty of often using the first-person pronoun. This is simply a means of effecting a more direct address to the reader. I would not like others to assume that this book is autobiographical, except in the broadest sense. I would love to practice what I preach, but I fall short more often than I succeed. I hope that I am not seen as demanding that others do spectacularly better than I can myself. In fact, I am not always sure what it means to be a good formator. With each new person that falls into our hands we often feel that we are beginning anew; we never lose our amateur status. Inevitably, relationships with some are smoother than with others, yet the benefit resulting from the relationship does not always seem to depend on this. We sometimes help most those with whom we are least at ease. Nevertheless, I hope that in discussing and developing a vast array of factors that have a bearing on a good formation process, I may provide one or two pointers that can be put into practice by different people in different situations. I have heard *The Imitation of Christ* quoted to the effect that if we could do better in one area every year, we would soon be perfect. So if this book offers a single useful suggestion to make formation more effective, writing it and reading it will be worthwhile.

It will soon become clear to the reader that, although I have attempted to speak of monastic formation in general terms, most of my experience is drawn from communities of men and from those living nearer to the contemplative pole of the Benedictine spectrum. I hope that my efforts to broaden the base of my remarks have made it possible for formators from other monastic traditions and beyond to identify with at least some of the experiences I describe. I am encouraged in this hope by the fact that, listening to formators from around the world, it has seemed to me that their experiences are quite similar, even though the environments in which they operate are unique and, therefore, different.

These reflections inevitably overlap with what I have written elsewhere, often at greater length on a particular point. I hope that I will be excused for referring to these treatments where they provide a fuller context to what I am describing here.

I once heard it said, correctly or not, that one goal of formation is to convince people that they are normal. One subsidiary objective of this book is to convince formators that, despite the particularity of their experiences, they too are approaching normality. In particular I hope that they will come to conclude that the difficulties, pressures, and failures that they have experienced are not uniquely theirs but shared by others working in the same field.

This book is dedicated to all formators, especially those with whom, at one time or another, it has been my privilege to work.

Chapter One

STIRRING THE POSSUM

Stir the possum, Australian: to instigate a debate on a controversial topic, especially in the public arena.

—Macquarie Dictionary

I am aware that there are different approaches and emphases in discussing monastic formation. If I undertake to clarify my own presuppositions in the matter, it is not because I wish to insist that these are nonnegotiable principles that exclude other ways of conceptualizing formation. These propositions are meant simply to add some precision to the discussion as it proceeds. I suppose I also want to convince you that it is a topic that is worth discussing at some length. Here is an initial list of fourteen themes about which I consider discussion timely.

1. *There is a need today for more explicit formation than was the case forty years ago.* In the past it sometimes happened that candidates slid naturally into the novitiate from an ambient Christian culture, a "good Catholic family," and more than a decade of Catholic education—often delivered by the very religious into whose ranks they were now seeking admission. They were, as it were, already in the system. It was just a matter of a relatively brief spell spent in learning the various domestic practices and rituals so that they could then be graduated as full-fledged participants in the monastic enterprise. Perhaps there was a chance of further theological or professional education, and that was it. Pastoral care of newcomers was often limited to giving general instruction, facilitating community living, and dealing with periodic outbreaks of vocational doubt or crisis.

Today, among those entering, such a smooth transition is rare and, if it does occur, may need to be regarded with an element of reserve. In the case of those whose commitment to Catholic values has never been threatened, care must be taken to distinguish between genuine innocence and the secret tyranny of repression. A majority of those interested in monasticism should be encouraged to view their premonastic life through a hermeneutic of discontinuity, even though it may have been relatively blameless. Probably they have lived a life of adult independence with responsibility for their own finances and a fair degree of freedom in their relationships and in expressing their sexuality. Between then and now there has been a conversion of greater or lesser magnitude, a different way of looking at the world and, gradually, a different way of conducting themselves. This process of change has led them to the monastery, but the need for change is not brought to a conclusion through their beginning monastic life. It will take years before the beliefs, attitudes, and values that they absorbed and practiced in growing up in a secular world are fully aligned with those of the monastery.

During this time they will need not only accompaniment and mentoring; they will need guidance, not only by exposure to good example and sound monastic doctrine but also sometimes by overt confrontation of new ways with old. This may involve two sensitive processes: usually it will be a matter of putting people right, of redirecting them (*correctio*, in the terminology of Saint Benedict); on occasion, however, the stronger medicine of *correptio* (rebuke) will be needed. For many of us these necessary interventions are difficult and taxing.[1] The whole reason for entering a monastery is to change one's life. Yet the strength of a person's instinctive resistance

---

1. As an aside, it may be said that perhaps we need to undertake a discussion of the pastoral role of "correction" (in whatever form it takes and however it is labeled) in our contemporary monastic world and what its virtual disappearance from the scene has meant. It is probably in this area more than any other that formators find themselves floundering.

to even small changes and challenges is not to be underestimated. The gap between pre-entry living and monastic living is wider now than it was generations ago. To become stable in one's monastic endeavor now demands a whole different mind-set. As a result, newcomers need much more help to negotiate this transition.

2. *What newcomers expect and hope to find is different from what it was two or four decades ago.* Here we do not have to rely on surmise or anecdotal evidence. In 2009 an exhaustive survey was conducted of four thousand persons who had entered the religious life in the United States in the preceding decade. Of course, the meaning of such surveys can be distorted by inherent bias in the researchers, the nonrepresentative profile of the respondents, or the failure of the analysts to find unassailable causal patterns. Moreover, it has to be remembered that, in this case, the respondents were those who entered. No guarantee is given that the same results would be obtained if the survey was retaken among those who persevere ten, twenty, or fifty years hence.

For what it is worth, the following is the official summary of the results, given by Sr. Mary Bendyna, the executive director of the Center for Applied Research in the Apostolate (CARA).

> The most successful institutes in terms of attracting and retaining new members at this time are those that follow a more traditional style of religious life in which members live together in community and participate in daily Eucharist, pray the Divine Office, and engage in devotional practices together. They also wear a religious habit, work together in common apostolates, and are explicit about their fidelity to the Church and the teachings of the Magisterium. All of these characteristics are especially attractive to the young people who are entering religious life today.[2]

---

2. The results are summarized in *Origins* 39.12 (2009). The full 406 pages of the report, which contains not only statistical summaries and conclusions but also the full text of all the responses to open-ended questions, can be found at

There are, of course, clear exceptions to this general trend, but these should not blind us to the fact that the tide may be moving in another direction. It is not always so easy for those of us who have gone through the stimulating years of post-conciliar renewal to realize that a new generation is calling for a new game-plan.

The renewal questions of today, however, are not those of the 1960s or the 1980s. For just as a generation that was young in religious life during the years immediately after the Council made its contribution to the work of renewal, there is no reason to believe that the current younger generation will not do the same.[3]

Monastic life, like the Church itself, is *semper reformanda*, always in a state of necessary reform. It follows that monastic formation needs continually to adapt to a different generation that is tentatively looking to seek and serve God in the age-old manner of monasticism. If in the last forty years we have not devoted energy to assessing and restructuring our formation processes, it probably means that they are hopelessly out of date—just the same old processes with any number of ad hoc fixes applied as time went by and, thus, in no way equipped to make the most of the possibilities that these times provide.

3. *Formation is a process that is not independent of persons.* I do not identify monastic formation with a set of principles, processes, and programs that are applied universally to all comers, year after year. This is a danger attached to the necessary task of attempting to formulate a written policy that is expected to be implemented everywhere, such as the *Ratio*

---

www.nrvc.net. For reflections on the meaning of the survey, see Seán Sammon, FMS, "Renewal of Religious Life in the US," *Origins* 40.19 (14 October 2010), 289–96. John Allen's review of trends likely to create the future Church notices some of the same characteristics. See John L. Allen, Jr., *The Future Church: How Ten Trends Are Revolutionizing the Catholic Church* (New York: Doudleday, 2009) 56.

3. Sammon, "Renewal," 290.

institutionis required by canon law. My experience has been that almost as soon as some sort of charter has been written, it has to be left aside. It is not always easy to accommodate reality with the ideal.[4] This is especially so when, as is common now, entrants include those who are older, more educated, more experienced, and, therefore, less homogeneous than previously anticipated. It becomes quickly apparent that the procedure that had been devised for a different demographic needs to be modified.

The same radical flexibility is required when entrants are few, or even solitary, and maybe separated from their nearest companions by a gap of some years. And we will soon learn from our own experience the truth of Robbie Burns's words: "The best laid schemes o' mice an' men gang aft a-gley." We all know how an unexpected family tragedy will necessitate an unforeseen change of direction in our interaction with those in our care and the consequent suspension of any intended agenda. Despite the infelicity of the term, I sometimes think that we should speak about "formations" rather than "formation," since the term describes processes that may be qualitatively distinct. For each person a different process needs to be imagined and implemented. In addition, formation has to be different for different communities and for different stages of a particular community's evolution.

4. *The real process of personal formation does not always coincide exactly with the canonical stages of initiation into monastic life.* Different persons move forward at different paces, and each follows a distinctive rhythm of development. Some, due to the internal or external dynamics of their situations, are forced to confront at a very early stage in their monastic life issues that, in most cases, need to be faced only much later, when coping-skill levels may be presumed to be higher. Others sail

---

4. As Goethe wrote, "The confusion of the real with the ideal never goes unpunished."

through their early years without any major crises, only to be floored in midlife by the sudden onset of problems more usually experienced much earlier on. In contrast to the variable rhythms that different people experience, the institutional process has stages terminating at pre-fixed dates. In particular, the duration of the novitiate and the period of temporary profession are determined by universal and particular law. In many communities it is inconvenient for persons to dally when they are due to move to the next stage, especially if they are part of a group.

What I would conclude from this observation, among other things, is that there needs to be some overarching agent of formation (usually this would be a superior) distinct from those immediately responsible for the various stages, with a supervisory role that would ensure both continuity and consistency in pastoral care, and with a concern for its maintenance in some form when the official stages of formation have been completed. The utility of this role of supervising and coordinating the work of different formators is probably one reason why canon law and most constitutions assume that the immediate responsibility for formation is best vested in a person distinct from the superior. Furthermore, in male monasteries it is important not to confuse monastic formation with formation for priestly ministry; there may be overlaps, but each will be more effective if its specificity is honored.

5. *Formation is more than an external training in the routines of the monastery*, including its spiritual practices. In such a relatively external approach, the newcomer is introduced or reintroduced to the daily life of the community including liturgy, prayer, *lectio divina*, common life, work, and study. It is taken for granted that if all these areas are covered, the internal dynamics of monastic growth will look after themselves. This sometimes happens, and for a time everything proceeds smoothly. Unless attention is paid to what is happening on the inside, however, it may be that the basic monastic values never

take root and the participation in monastic practices does not yield the anticipated fruit. Many of those who eventually leave are people who have, on the surface, been models of observance; their departure signals that they probably never internalized the values inherent in the practices.

Most monastic observances will have their intended effect only if their meaning is apparent. Often this will call for explicit instruction. For example, *lectio divina* is an art that requires more than simply knowing how to read the Bible. Plonking a novice down in front of the Scriptures is a start, but it is no more than that. *Lectio* is an activity that requires a measure of spiritual literacy as well as of intelligent reading. It demands a capacity to read the echoes of the text in the heart. This sensitivity is developed slowly, perhaps facilitated by a crisis or two, and often only with careful mentoring. As with *lectio*, the meaning of many monastic observances is not self-evident; many newcomers necessarily have to struggle creatively with compliance. Too much insistence on external conformity can subvert this useful process of arriving at a working solution. When this is not allowed to happen, the result is often resentment, both in the present and in the future. Without neglecting external training, a certain priority needs to be given to ensuring that the person's beliefs and values are keeping pace with visible behavior.

6. *A vocation is not something superadded to one's nature but its most complete expression.* Therefore, the whole concern in accompanying a person through the early stages of monastic probation is to discover whether there is an incipient harmony between what monastic life has to offer and the deeper strands of the newcomer's personality.[5] The implicit principle behind

---

5. Many of those seeking to clarify their sense of vocation have found helpful the first part of Parker J. Palmer's *Let Your Life Speak: Listening for the Voice of Vocation* (San Francisco: Jossey-Bass, 2000). The point that he makes very strongly is that following a vocation is not a matter of attempting to become what

formation is "Become what you are!" Monastic asceticism has no other goal than to facilitate the expression of the person's deepest potentiality. This will involve, in turn, the renunciation of external sources of alienation, the consistent preference for what Merton has termed "the deep self" over the "superficial self," and, eventually, at the level of contemplation, the complete evacuation of the superficial self in order to become transparent to God.[6]

The deep self is the sphere in which fundamental desire operates, the ontological dynamism that is named by Christian authors the "desire for God." The formator's task is to help the person to deal with this inner dynamism: to isolate Desire from spurious incarnations (desires), to provide a language to describe Desire, to remove what inhibits or distorts Desire, to make room for Desire to grow, and to teach Desire how to shape behavior.[7] This is a much more profound process than merely instructing newcomers how to perform the practices prescribed by the Rule, and it is an endeavor that may, in different modes, span several decades. Entering into monastic formation, in this sense, is to begin a lifelong journey; it is crucial that the beginner is not sent off in a wrong direction. Starting on the right track means breaking with a more or less inauthentic (but not necessarily bad) past and rebuilding one's life on the solid base of authentic selfhood. This leads to the conclusion long known to experience that there is no substitute for a good initial formation.

7. It is never quite certain what degree of human development or maturity is necessary to begin monastic formation. It is fairly obvi-

---

you want to become, nor what others want you to become or think you should become, but becoming what you are, choosing a way of life that accords best with your nature.

6. The reader will recognize this progression as reflecting the triple renunciation about which Abba Paphnutius spoke in Cassian's third conference. The same progression is taught by Evagrius of Pontus.

7. I use a capital letter for "Desire" when I mean the ontological desire for God.

ous that the period of formation will not achieve its specific goals if it is wholly consumed by dealing with developmental issues that should have been handled before entry. Since maturity is often a function of the quality of choices made, those whose life has not presented them with a wide range of choices may not have built the strength of character that they will eventually need to persevere in monastic life.[8] Admittedly, some of these issues may be triggered only by the more intense environment of the monastery and were not foreseeable. But, normally, their existence should have been at least partially uncovered during initial history taking or in psychological testing, if this was done before entry. Nobody is ever perfectly mature at the beginning; it is a question, rather, of having attained a critical mass that will enable the process of specifically monastic formation to proceed.

Sometimes it may seem worthwhile to set aside the postulancy as a time for processing the events and experiences of a person's life and coming to the point of a warm self-acceptance and a confidence that will boost the effectiveness of monastic formation.[9] There will always be some overlap of human and monastic formation as the person's experience broadens in monastic life and new challenges are faced. In every case, however, a noninfallible practical judgment will need to be made about whether a person has sufficient maturity to profit from spiritual and monastic guidance.

---

8. The psychological health needed to internalize monastic values is consistent with a relative freedom from the dominance of needs and instincts, especially unconscious ones. This freedom must be coupled with a true sense of self and the boldness of normal adult self-assertion. It is normal for persons to regress on first entering a monastery; it is important that formators encourage them to return quickly to adulthood. It needs to be remembered that the monastic regimen is framed for committed adults, just as monastic education programs are adult education.

9. One way of doing this is by engaging in a structured autobiography.

8. *The best environment in which to begin monastic life is total immersion*, as it is with learning a foreign language. Those who come as disciples have a need to encounter one who is prepared to be a master. An easygoing approach may be rationalized as a form of prudent gradualism,[10] "tempering the cold wind to the shorn sheep." But, in practice, it often sets a precedent by which individuals remain in control of their own lives, and they unknowingly continue to be driven by their particular passions, neuroses, and superego, thus effectively neutralizing the purposes of this period of transition and change.[11]

Most arrive at a monastery expecting some restrictions; it is a kindness when these are spelled out clearly instead of leaving newcomers in a quandary of unspoken expectations and invisible boundaries. This prescriptiveness is no more than Saint Benedict proposes when he states that the beginning of monastic life cannot but be somewhat restrictive (RB Prol. 47-48). It is especially important to be clear about such rules and to give suitable explanations in a community where there are seniors who seem rather cavalier about complying with the details of observance. Newcomers notice this nonconformity, and they want to know why.

9. *It should not be quickly assumed that newcomers know what is best for them* and should thus be allowed to pick and choose among monastic values and observances, perhaps in the manner of some of the more eclectic seniors in the community. Monastic growth is growth in self-transcendence. We need to

---

10. John Gray coined the phrase "doctrinaire *laisser-faire*" to characterize this approach.

11. This self-will can sometimes be demonstrated by expressions of apparent fervor in which personal devotions are abundantly superadded to the monastic regime or by penitential practices adopted (such as food restriction or sleep deprivation) that may upset the basic monastic equilibrium.

have "the courage to teach"—to use Parker Palmer's phrase.[12] Once, in visiting an International Yoga Federation ashram, I was surprised to meet several persons who had previously been in seminaries and religious communities and were attracted to this stricter form of life precisely because of its discipline. They were there because they had confidence in the swami's ability to teach them to meditate and so to take them beyond their limits into zones previously unexperienced. They felt that their previous formation was too lax.

Western monasticism is a sound tradition and has much to offer; there is no reason why we should not be confident in communicating its wisdom to those who come to us. Sometimes novices or, more especially, those in temporary vows accept the tradition but doubt the credentials of those assigned them as formators. They may try to teach themselves through books, or they may attach themselves to another member of the community or go over the formator's head to the superior. These are delicate situations, and we will return to discuss them later on. It may be that these are tactics to circumvent the challenge of an assigned relationship rather than a sincere search for guidance.

10. *Formation comes primarily through sustained personal interaction*—with the formator, with the superior, and with members of the community. Formation gatherings, distance education, imported teachers, and reading lists cannot replace this long-term personal contact. This is because formation is not achieved solely by pouring in extraneous material. It also requires bringing into clearer consciousness what is known only obscurely. This is especially the case in monastic communities, where newcomers are soon exposed to all the quirks of human nature in a group that is not handpicked for its formative potential. Such uncensored interaction often brings

---

12. Parker J. Palmer, *The Courage to Teach: Exploring the Inner Landscape of a Teacher's Life* (San Francisco: Jossey-Bass, 1998).

to the surface tendencies and sensitivities hitherto unnoticed. Unscripted conversation invites newcomers to speak from the heart what has previously been unspoken.

It is hoped that community members are able to welcome this even when it seems to contradict a person's approved public image. Simultaneously being heard by oneself and by another person strongly affirms the reality of an emerging identity that will serve as the lifelong engine of monastic development. This is not something that can be achieved quickly or in accordance with a preplanned timetable. Often such disclosure comes outside formal interview sessions, in the day-to-day dealings that constitute the common life. A practical consequence is that formators especially need to have ample time available for leisurely listening. This is probably why canon law insists that they not be given other occupations.[13]

11. *Formators must be prepared to teach as much by the quality of their lives as by formal instruction.* One way in which formators win souls is by embodying monastic practice in their daily living. This is the challenge of modeling.[14] Ideally, the whole community participates in this task, but the reality is a little different. As we all know, there is a tendency to take shortcuts as the decades roll by, and the behavior of the more senior members of the community can sometimes contradict what newcomers are being taught. Formators serve as the primary interface between newcomers and the community. It is from those who have immediate dealings with them that newcomers absorb monastic attitudes. It is easier for newcomers to appreciate monastic values when these are embedded in a

---

13. Can. 651.3, CIC, states, "Those in charge of the formation of novices are to be members who have been carefully prepared, and who are not burdened with other tasks, so that they may discharge their office fruitfully and in a stable fashion."

14. See M. Casey, "Modelling: A Challenge for Formators," *Tjurunga* 75 (November 2008) 18–30.

living that is honest, healthy, and contented. Obviously, giving good example may sometimes seem burdensome for the formators, but it is the most potent means by which they can ensure some measure of credibility for their verbal teaching.

12. *The need for adaptation is not restricted to newcomers; the community also must change.* Welcoming a new community member has a dynamic different from welcoming a guest. Although the postulant and novice remain in a transitional stage of probation for an extended period, they become part of the community.[15] Cynical seniors may gaze upon the new recruit and mutter to themselves, "How long will this one last?"; nevertheless those who enter come with the intention of staying permanently. It is important that they be allowed to feel at home, that their uniqueness be recognized and respected—even as they struggle to cope with the daunting task of fitting into a community that has lived together for a long time and has developed its own quirks and customs. Seniors should know that their behavior is being observed as the potential end product of a long monastic life. They are, as it were, living advertisements for the fact that monasticism can deliver what it promises in its promotional literature—or not, as the case may be. Good example seems like an old-fashioned concept nowadays, but the conscious attempt to give good example can often serve as a spur to recovering some of our own fervor. Those communities that have not accepted newcomers for many years will testify that a certain ennui or slackness often follows long years of sterility. With new life comes new energy to rise up out of the rut.

---

15. For example, OCSO Constitution 6 states, "The community is composed of brothers who have made profession in it, novices and others who have been admitted into the community on probation, and [conventual] oblates." Those still on probation are not, of course, members of the conventual chapter.

13. *Opinions about formation that are based on anecdotes are not always reliable.* All of us have heard stories about "the good old days" and their splendid outcomes. The fact that Fr. Abel has never done any serious courses in theology nor received any regular spiritual direction and yet is a wonderful monk proves nothing. Nor does simple-minded Sr. Bibiana's absolute dedication to her work. That Br. Crispin may have spent his novitiate in a power struggle with his formator and yet survived to become a useful community member is a wonder to be admired rather than imitated. It is not prudent to draw normative conclusions on the basis of incomplete knowledge and superficial judgments. We rarely know the inner face of a person's story, and we will never know the difference that a more effective formation may have made to some of our grand old characters. Their struggles deserve better of us than cheap shots in a political affray. Often one encounters seniors who shake their heads and wonder why there is all this fuss about formation. They think that newcomers should simply grit their teeth and "live the life."[16]

14. *The quality of formation given is not necessarily indicated by the proportion of novices or juniors who graduate.* A formation that brings them to the point of realizing that they do not have a monastic vocation is a successful formation, even though the outcome is disappointing to the community and to the formators. Sometimes a high level of affective bonding with the formator and/or the failure to unearth and confront

---

16. "One of the things you should beware of, first of all, is the idea that the religious, the contemplative, does not need any formation or education. We know this is wrong, but it has been very strongly emphasized in the past and we have all suffered from it: don't read too much; don't learn too much; don't let them get their hands on too much theology—it is bad for them. Philosophy too is bad for them, and what they don't know won't hurt them." Thomas Merton, "Prayer, Tradition, and Experience," in *Thomas Merton in Alaska: The Alaskan Conferences, Journals, and Letters* (New York: New Directions, 1989) 119.

negative tendencies may disguise the fact that that a person is not truly called to this way of life. The truth of the matter becomes clearer some years later as the person becomes progressively detached from the integrity of monastic observance and then leaves.

* * *

Not everyone understands the term "monastic formation" in the same sense. In any contentious discussion of monastic formation no advance toward agreement is possible because those involved are envisaging different realities or, at least, approaching the topic from different angles. Without wishing to eliminate all differences of opinion, it can be helpful to arrive at a common language in which the issues can be discussed more effectively. In this way a working consensus can be formed, and the value of complementary positions can be appreciated.

Those old enough to remember Avery Dulles's landmark contribution to ecclesiology, *Models of the Church*,[17] will recognize the source of what I am going to say. Dulles's basic premise is that one potential cause of disagreement in theological debate derives from the fact that different people are using the same word with an entirely different meaning. Just as the terms "church" or "revelation" can be used equivocally, so too can "monastic formation." When we discuss "formation," are we all talking about the same reality? To speak about different models of monastic formation is not a question of proposing *alternative* models. The models that I enumerate all operate simultaneously: each is real; each is important. Confusion begins when we fail to distinguish between them. When we

---

17. This point is developed in M. Casey, "Models of Monastic Formation," *Tjurunga* 45 (1993) 3–31. The article was reprinted in *An Unexciting Life: Reflections on Benedictine Spirituality* (Petersham, MA: St. Bede's Publications, 2005) 361–405. See Avery Dulles, *Models of the Church* (Garden City: Doubleday, 1974). See also his *Models of Revelation* (Garden City: Doubleday, 1983).

talk about formation, it seems important to me that we specify to which aspect of formation we are referring.

In general terms we may speak of "formation" as being either the work of God or the work of the community or the work of those designated by the community to act as formators. In fact, all these formative influences operate simultaneously. Nevertheless, it is almost inevitable that when we speak of formation, we will be thinking not of all three channels together but especially of one. Whatever policy we devise will be based on that emphasis. In the chapters that follow I will discuss formation first as the effect of God's grace, then as different aspects of the work of the community, and then as the particular responsibility of those nominated to act as formators. Having laid this foundation, we may be in a position to reflect more clearly on the issues that constitute the challenge of formation today.

Chapter Two

THE WORK OF THE HOLY SPIRIT

Just as we look for God's touch in the vocation story of those who come to us, so too, throughout life, the principal agent in the stabilization of a vocation and in the sanctification of the person is the ongoing action of God through the Holy Spirit. There can be no dispute about this, although sometimes we tend to forget it. This means, in brief, that the more monks and nuns make room in their lives for the mindful celebration of liturgy, for prayer and *lectio divina*, the more likely will be their progress in monasticity and their perseverance. This is so obvious that it scarcely warrants saying.

All monastic development builds on the foundation of baptism and occurs within an ecclesial and sacramental context.[1] In accompanying those who are in the years of transition, it is easy to concentrate too exclusively on personal struggles and the dynamics of socialization into the community. These are real and urgent issues, but they may not attain resolution without the reality of grace working in the person as the years pass. Perhaps in years gone by we have paid too little attention to what may be termed the "psychological" aspects of formation. Now, however, there is a danger of going to the opposite extreme.

This leads, inevitably, to an emphasis on promoting efforts to iron out inconsistencies and to become integrated human beings. This is a praiseworthy, necessary, and, sometimes, urgent enterprise, but there is more to monastic life than this.

---

1. See M. Casey, "Sacramentality and Monastic Consecration," *Word and Spirit* 18 (1998) 27–48; reprinted in *An Unexciting Life: Reflections on Benedictine Spirituality* (Petersham, MA: St. Bede's Publications, 2005) 263–85.

Respectfully considering even the holiest among our brothers and sisters reminds us that the task is never complete this side of eternity. Monastic life makes more sense when it is seen as an ever-increasing reliance on the mercy of God. Self-improvement, as desirable as it seems, must take second place to this. Perhaps the tinges of a mild form of Pelagianism some have found in the writings of John Cassian can serve as a warning not to forget grace, no matter how urgent and important more immediate issues seem.

The monastery is the house of God, and not only strangers are affected by its numinous power. It is true that we quickly become habituated to this so that it is easy to lose an awareness of God's presence in the monastery. But a love for the place and a sense of its sacredness are potent forces in bringing a monastic vocation to its fruition. We can see this from the first and last steps of Saint Benedict's ladder of humility. We begin with the laborious effort of living under the eye of God, and we end by finding God wherever we are: "at the Work of God, in the oratory, in the monastery, in the garden, on the road, in the field" (RB 7.63). The transition from looking to seeing, from seeking to finding, is emblematic of monastic life as a whole. As the decades pass, everything becomes imbued with the divine presence.

Bernard of Clairvaux was convinced that the monastery is, above all, a place where grace can be found and spiritual life nurtured. He advises us to walk about carefully in case we trip on the angels, because they are everywhere.[2] This is a holy place that, if we open ourselves to its energy, leaves its imprint on us:

> This community is made up not of the wicked but of saints, religious persons, those who are full of grace and worthy of blessing. You come together to hear the word of God, you gather to sing praise, to pray, to offer adoration. This is a

---

2. Bernard of Clairvaux, QH 12:6; SBO 4, 460.

consecrated assembly, pleasing to God and familiar with the angels. Therefore, brothers, stand fast in reverence, stand with care and devotion of mind, especially in the place of prayer and in this school of Christ where the Spirit is heard [*auditorium spirituale*].[3]

People enter monasteries because there is a resonance between the holiness they perceive there and the deepest aspirations of their being. They come in the hope that somehow their spiritual lives will be nurtured, that they will experience a more profound union with God. In most cases it is a hope, not a demand; it is not equally explicit in all, but the desire to connect more closely with the spiritual world seems almost universal.

If someone's conscious motivation for coming to the monastery has been to seek God, it seems sensible to use this fundamental desire as an engine of growth, in the human sphere as well as spiritually. There may be other currents operating within this primary motivation: the search for safe structures, the quest for a perfect parent, flight from interior tumult blamed on "the world," even some elevation in social status. There may be a romantic coloring to the attraction. They may see themselves swanning around medieval cloisters in voluminous robes or performing some service that wins universal acclaim. Behind these superficialities there can be something real. Saint Benedict's question remains relevant: Are they genuinely seeking God? If not now, how will they ever come to that point?

Desire is what makes us human. It is the most dynamic part of our being. It is desire that propels us toward God and thus is the principal shaper of our monastic or spiritual life. Alas, this fundamental desire can be subverted or diverted. It can attach itself to lesser goods or use the pursuit of the highest ideals as an unconscious disguise for less worthy motivations. Because of this potential ambivalence, it is necessary that,

---

3. Bernard of Clairvaux, JB 1; SBO 5, 176.

especially in the early years, a person's fundamental desire not be ignored.

The question is asked in the traditional ritual of initiation, "What do you seek?" This question needs to be posed again and again throughout life. In fact, it could be argued that the most important task in formation is to keep this question before the person's mind. Vocation is embedded in the experience of desire for God; the more fully this desire has access to consciousness, the more God's formative action is given scope to operate.

There is more. Saint Benedict speaks about monastic life in terms of participating through patience in the paschal mystery (RB Prol. 50). A wholehearted embrace of this form of life depends totally on the vigor of a person's faith and devotion. If the monastery is conceived as an expression of the mystery of the Church, then all that relates to the monastery's life is invested with a sacred character and needs to be dealt with as such. This means learning to assess situations with the eye of faith. Those with much experience in accompanying others are aware that in times of crisis it is only faith that helps people reach a creative solution. Those whose faith is weak quickly buckle under the assault of contrary winds. It may seem an odd thing to say, but it is only a vigorous spiritual life that will keep people afloat in difficult times. And, believe it or not, it is possible to live many years in a monastery without a vigorous spiritual life.

Let me insist. When I place an emphasis on the work of God in a person's monastic development, I am not suggesting that we need pay little attention to a person's history or to the level of consistency between aspiration and behavior. This will become evident in later chapters. Nor am I saying that there is no place for psychological assessment and counseling. The point being emphasized is that, while making use of whatever aids the social sciences and our own common sense provide, there remains an element of mystery in individual stories that can be explained only by reference to the action of grace.

I recognize that viewing formation principally as the work of God may provide a pretext for reducing the formative task to that of accompaniment, standing on the sidelines and allowing God to get on with the task. That is far from my intention since such a hands-off approach will leave many personal, professional, and communitarian issues unaddressed and the person's life less happy than it could have been. I am suggesting that a monastic life that has the capacity to bring a person very close to God is not primarily the work of human formation. It is, above all, God's work. As Saint Benedict says at the end of his chapter on humility, this is what the Lord manifests in a person's life through the ongoing action of the Holy Spirit. Many of the minor goals for which we may strive as formators may never be realized, and many of the encumbrances that we have sought to eliminate remain strong until the end. In the final analysis these imperfections seem not to detract from the beauty of what God has achieved in the life of those who have lived their days in the radiance of the divine presence.

The School of Christ

Saint Benedict describes the monastery as "a school of the Lord's service" (RB Prol. 45), and other authors use terms like "school of Christ" and "school of love." The point being made in all these designations is that we come to the monastery to learn. The question may be asked, "What do we expect to learn in a monastery?" We learn many things, obviously, but the specific monastic learning is how to enter into union with God, how to live responsively to God's grace, how to reshape our lives so that in all things God is glorified. We come to the monastery in order to grow spiritually. The monastery ultimately is a school of contemplation, but this is God's gift and not the fruit of any human skill or the result of effective training. We prepare people to receive this gift by encouraging their practice of prayer, by helping them to have well-formed consciences, and, above all, by insisting on their sensitivity to the stirrings of the Holy Spirit. Even given these conditions, there is no guarantee that God will work according to our timetable. But normally, in the last quadrant of life, we can expect to see the flowering of grace.

This spiritual growth comes about by living our life under the guidance of the Gospel (RB Prol. 21) and never moving away from Christ's teaching (RB Prol. 50). It means—using the language of Clement of Alexandria—taking Christ as our "pedagogue" and desiring to become more and more like him.

Monastic formators are not gurus seeking to mold disciples in their own image and likeness or according to a particular image they have in their heads. Saint Benedict tells the abbot very clearly that his role is to be a channel of Christ's wisdom, not the propagator of his own. "Therefore the abbot is not to teach or establish anything as policy or to give instruction outside the Lord's precept [*extra præceptum Domini*]" (RB 2.4). The abbot speaks with the voice of Christ not because he replaces Christ but because he makes it his primary concern in all things to act and to respond as Christ did, to be a carrier of Christ's word.

The same applies to the formator. Formation is not a matter of imposing personal preferences on others. The ultimate purpose of formation is to lead those who come to us into a more direct and more intense relationship with Christ, such as will outlast by several decades their early years of formation. The formator is, like John the Baptist, a person with the theme song, "I must decrease so that Christ may increase" (John 3:30).

There is a sense in which the monastic *conversatio* replaces the formator when the period of formation has finished and when the sense of vocation has stabilized. The mature monk or nun draws consolation, support, guidance, challenge, and correction from *lectio divina*, from the Liturgy of the Hours, and from the other ordinary exercises of the monastic day by which contact with Christ is maintained. We are called to live mindful of Christ's presence in the sick (RB 36.1), in the stranger (RB 53.1), in the superior (RB 2.2), and in all whom we encounter in the course of a day. This awareness is the fruit of grace, of fidelity to grace, and, in some way, of a good formation. It is, as John Cassian reminds us in his first conference, a matter of keeping our eyes fixed on the ultimate goal.

In a world of many distractions, people enter monasteries with a view to concentrating their lives on the one thing necessary. The greatest service that the community can do is to keep reminding them of the ultimate purpose of the choice they have made. This means asking the question that Saint Benedict asks a priest entrant: "Friend, why have you come?" (RB 60.3; cf. Matt 26:50). Saint Bernard, we read, used to ask the same question of himself: "For the purpose of keeping guard over his heart and maintaining the constancy of his resolve, he often had these words in his mouth, 'Bernard, Bernard, why have you come?'"[4]

It is important to keep this ultimate goal in sight, otherwise newcomers will continue to live in state of distractedness with little capacity for enduring the ambiguities and trials that everyone experiences. In this view, those who assist others to enter into the fullness of the monastic vocation are not trying to accomplish anything except to keep them on target so that they may be constantly directed by their consciences and by their particular sense of vocation. This means, in practice, bringing persons into the fullest possible harmony with the purifying and simplifying action of the Holy Spirit (RB 7.70). For this to occur, a whole lot of learning has to happen, with all the pangs that normally accompany it.

This openness to divine formation occurs most explicitly at the time of *lectio divina*, and so, in a sense, the whole of monastic formation can be summed up in accompanying newcomers in their daily encounter with Christ in *lectio*. The art of sacred reading is not self-evident, especially to the Internet generation, and much patient guidance is often required. In *lectio* many will encounter those negative tendencies within

---

4. Bernard of Clairvaux, *Vita Prima*, 1:4, 19; PL 185, 238b.

themselves that make monastic life difficult and their perseverance uncertain. Once these come to the surface, they can be dealt with elsewhere. If novices and juniors are well-formed to *lectio*, they will soon begin to find there a source of strength and good cheer and the most potent source of perseverance.

The work of formation consists of many different and sometimes contrary tasks and can occasion a certain degree of anxiety. Without in any way dispensing ourselves from these concerns, it is necessary always to keep in mind that it is God who will bring to perfection the good work that has begun. While we accompany those in our care by listening and accepting, we need also to accompany them by prayer, which Saint Benedict regards as a more potent remedy than our more overt pastoral interventions (RB 28.4). At the same time, we need to keep reminding God of our own inadequacies in helping others and even in coping with our own problems. When efforts to form others come adrift from prayer, trouble may be expected.

Chapter Three

THE COMMUNITY'S WORK

Even until late in life persons formed in different monasteries often bear the visible imprint of their initial matrix. This can be seen not only in the style of their outward habits but also in the specific coloring of the beliefs and values that shape their intimate spirituality. Exactly how this dynamic works is worth examining.

From a sociological point of view, following a suggestion of Jürgen Habermas, we can say that there are three main channels of influence from the group to the individual: involvement in the characteristic tasks of the group, internalizing its beliefs and values, and participating progressively in its power structures.[1] At first the new arrival is told simply to do what everyone else does, on the understanding that the reason for these activities will soon become clear, partly by being involved in them and partly by seeking answers to the questions that this participation arouses. As persons become more comfortable in a group, they begin to view things from the perspective of the group and to use the argot of the group. In speaking about the group, for example, they begin to use "we" in place of "they." Then, to the extent that they demonstrate their adherence to group values, they are given responsibilities in the exercise of which they are confirmed in their appreciation and understanding of the beliefs and values that make the group distinctive.

In monastic life, from the very beginning, we ask newcomers to take their part in the liturgy and in various domestic routines and to participate in the regimen that has been designed for

---

1. See M. Casey, "The Formative Influence of the Benedictine Community," *Tjurunga* 14 (1977) 7–26.

those newly entered. We teach them about the values of monastic tradition by word and example, and we invite them to make these values their own.² We progressively put them in positions where they have to exercise some discretionary authority, ideally with the help of a mentor or supervisor, so that their reception of the tradition is active rather than merely passive. In this way, by contributing to the process of objectivating the core values they have internalized, they become an integral part of the group, transmitting the charism to the next generation in a way that is faithful to the past and yet unique, since it embodies the special character of the persons involved. We are not forming people with a view to their being perpetuators of a uniform and static tradition that never changes. We are involving them in a dynamic process of giving and receiving in which it is by passing on what they have received to others that they most fully make the tradition their own. This is the responsibility of all, and it seems that Saint Benedict recognized this.

---

2. The process of internalization goes something like this. Having accepted to act as the community acts, the newcomer gradually accepts the key beliefs and values of the community, grafting them seamlessly onto previously cherished values. There is a meeting of two cultures or value systems, one personal, the other social, optimally leading to a common horizon; the newcomer comes to see things as the community sees them. The "new" values and the "old" values conjoin in the newcomer, serving as daily basis of his action and response. This "fusion of horizons," the ability to blend "old" and "new" values, is the surest guarantee of a monastic vocation. According to Luigi Rulla, internalization occurs when individuals accept influence because the induced behavior is congruent with their value systems (primary socialization and previous socializations); when the content of the induced attitude or behavior is intrinsically rewarding; when the attitude or behavior does not depend on social pressure; when it has become part of a personal approach to life; and when the internalized attitude or behavior is not dependent on a gratifying relationship with a mentor (identification), nor on approval-disapproval processes within the community (compliance). Luigi M. Rulla, Franco Imoda, Joyce Ridick, *Psychological Structure and Vocation: A Study of the Motivations for Entering and Leaving the Religious Life* (Dublin: Villa Books, 1979) 91.

Thus, in Saint Benedict's vision, every member of the community, by virtue of seniority or age, shares in the educative function that, in the classical perspective of cenobitism, was reserved exclusively to the abbot and his officers. In a still wider sense, the chapter "On Good Zeal" attributes to the life of fraternal relations in charity the purifying and sanctifying effects that the Master saw as the characteristic of ascesis pursued under the direction of an abbot.[3]

The formative role of the community is crucial to the development of a monastic vocation, but it will happen only to the extent that a community consciously accepts its corporate responsibility, with all the limitations on individual lifestyle that this involves. One of the most recurrent difficulties that formators face in caring for newcomers is that the newcomers' closer observation of the selfish and individualistic behavior of some of the middle-ranking seniors can undermine their confidence in the values and practices they are being asked to adopt. The community is formative, and so it needs to take this responsibility seriously. The 2009 CARA demonstrated that newcomers care about the quality of the lifestyle; it follows that they are disenchanted and disedified by the slipshod habits of those who should know better. The fact is that the community is forming newcomers, for weal or for woe, whether it is conscious of it or not.

There are three main channels by which community influence is communicated to those who enter: by handing on the particular charism of the community, by training them in the practical living of that charism as it occurs locally, and by providing them with an education in the specific beliefs and values of monastic life. All three media are important, and they need to operate jointly.

---

3. Adalbert de Vogüé, *Community and Abbot in the Rule of Saint Benedict* (Kalamazoo, MI: Cistercian Publications, 1988) 431.

Transmission of the Charism

God's formative action in the depths of the soul is complemented by the human activity by which unformed spiritual aspirations are gradually given concrete expression. The "charism" of a religious order is not abstract; it is incarnated in the lives of brothers and sisters who have consented to be formed by it. These are people who have received the talent and are able to pass it on with interest added. Some might remember the catechetical dictum of the 1960s: "Religion is not taught; it is caught." The same applies to the process of transmitting the monastic spirit from one generation to the next.

For this generative process to happen, conditions apply on both sides. On the part of those who enter, there must be a willingness to be formed by the community, overcoming contrarian tendencies, adolescent rebellion, contentiousness, and compulsive singularity. This requires a substantial level of openness and trust in the community. This topic will be discussed in detail in the next chapter.

On the part of the community members, there must be a visible joy and confidence in their vocation and the willingness to give good example. This means a zeal for maintaining the objective integrity of the monastic *conversatio* rather than trimming and reshaping it to suit subjective needs, inclinations, or preferences. Such practice not only provides good example for the newcomers but also helps the quality of our own monastic observance to improve. It seems to me that this is precisely the object of the vow of *conversatio morum*.

On first appearances it may seem that communities are run by middle-aged mavericks who bustle around the monastery making decisions and getting things done. In God's providence they are at a time of life when they have the energy and interest to do this, and the monastery benefits greatly from their efforts. For all their visibility (and perhaps self-importance), they are far from being the heart of the community. This privilege often belongs to a few older persons, the spiritual seniors about whom Saint Benedict speaks, who have passed beyond ambition for executive functions and are content with the faithful living of the *conversatio* and the practice of the commonplace virtues. These persons often have considerable impact on newcomers through their humanity, their gentleness, and their fervor. Often they serve as sources of comfort, counsel, and inspiration outside the formal structures of formation. Sometimes in new foundations or where tasks exceed available personnel, the importance of such bridge-builders and models is overlooked. It is vital that those new to monastic life be given some idea of the end product so that they are not compelled to discover new roads for themselves. By following "the common rule of the monastery and the example of those more advanced" (RB 7.55), they are able to run along well-trodden paths that lead in the direction they themselves have chosen to travel.

The respect spontaneously generated by mellow seniority is an attestation of holiness, however homely its expression. This is not merely a question of age or years in monastic life. It is a mysterious quality by which some people seem to embody some essential features of the monastic vocation and make them visible. The wonderful thing is that the holiness of each member of the community is unique. Listen to what Bernard of Clairvaux says of the members of a monastic community. He begins by praising their unity; however, he then shows that this unity consists not in uniformity but in each person responding to the particular grace that God has given and living by it. Within the round of activities punctuated by the Liturgy of the Hours and the other events of common life, there is scope for each person to live with flair:

> You will see one of them weeping for his sins, another rejoicing in the praise of God, another tending the needs of all, and another giving instruction to the rest. Here is one who is at prayer and another at reading; here is one who is compassionate and another who inflicts penalties for sins. This one is aflame with love and that one is valiant in humility. This one remains humble when everything goes

well and this other one does not lose his nerve in difficulties. This one works very hard in active tasks, the other finds quiet in the practice of contemplation.[4]

Nobody has all possible gifts—since some of them are not easily compatible—but where there is a corporate witness to the pluriform attractiveness of monastic *conversatio*, the sound formation of those who enter is almost certainly assured. It is through such spiritual seniors that life is passed from one generation to the next. This is a gift of the Spirit, a charism given for the benefit of the community.

On the other hand, it seems to me that a community will cease to have a positive formative impact if it has lost its vision and no longer has the confidence to be prescriptive in describing its daily life or in setting reasonable boundaries. If common projects crumble due to rampant individualism, all that is left is a minimum of basic observances that are judged to be secondary to each one's private pursuits. I cannot see that a community could be said to be formative that describes itself in the following manner: "The community life is loosely structured and flexible in order to develop and utilize the talents of each individual and avoid any risk of de-personalization."[5]

It sometimes happens when communities cease to attract new members that a spirit of "live and let live" develops. These are comfortable and unchallenging places to live; few demands are made on the members, each goes about his or her own business, and any project that would require consensus is avoided. At the level of community there is stagnation, even though the members may seem happy enough and community parties are well attended. Through pervasive indifference, leadership is reduced to mere management, concentrating

---

4. Bernard of Clairvaux, Div 42:4; SBO 6a, 258.
5. *Your Choice: A Handbook for Young Adults Seeking Their Place in a Lifetime Ministry* (Chicago: National Religious Vocation Conference, 1992) 61.

on an effort to keep the peace. The status quo becomes paramount, and no one seems to recognize that community standards are not remaining constant but are slowly declining. Such communities do not attract vocations because there is no fundamental culture of vocation attraction, even though time, energy, and money may be invested in trying to recruit new members. This is because what attracts most candidates (85 percent in the 2009 CARA survey) are existing members' joy, down-to-earth nature, and commitment. Such qualities are not apparent in nongenerative communities.

All is not lost. One of the gratifying qualities of monastic tradition is its apparent capacity to leapfrog a generation and to rekindle the flame that had been almost extinguished by lukewarmness. Here we can think of the many movements of reform within the Benedictine tradition. Although most of them espoused a more exigent life, their single-mindedness was such that new entrants were abundant. Perhaps we need to consider whether the best means of attracting vocations is improving the quality of our community lifestyle and the visible fervor of our commitment to fundamental monastic values.

Training in the Way of Life

If it is true that the community is a local embodiment of the Church, then it is a channel of grace to those who come into contact with it and especially for those who are its members. There are, however, practical matters to be faced in easing the transition of newcomers into the already established culture of the community. No matter how accommodating communities are, a great deal of acceptance accorded to new members is dependent on their willingness to fit in with the way things are done, learning how to take their part unobtrusively in the everyday activities that characterize community life. Since the conventions and manners of a monastic community are quite different from anything entrants may have experienced previously, they are in need of a certain amount of explicit instruction.

At an obvious level the neophyte needs to learn the usual community and liturgical customs. For example, there are many good-living people entering monasteries today who do not have a clue about either the theory or practice of the *Angelus* as it is observed in many communities. Likewise, they may need some instruction in chant. It is likely that the work they are given will be unfamiliar, and so they will have to acquire some knowledge of how it is done locally. Communal living may be a new experience for many, and some initiation into its sensitivities may be required.

For many entering the monastery today a certain amount of bodily training is necessary. For some it will involve adapting to a different climate. For most it will be a matter of gradually changing their biorhythms. For nearly all who come, staying up late at night is second nature; a monastery with its rule of early rising will demand that they retire earlier, and so their sleep patterns will have to change. The same is true of food; adaptation to the quantity, quality, pace, and schedule of monastic eating will be necessary. To the extent that they are involved in manual work, some hitherto undiscovered sets of muscles will be exercised. They may have to be taught the importance of rhythm in physical activity; without it they will quickly become weary.

Nowadays there is some discussion of the notion of "flow"—a manner of acting and working in which body and mind cooperate so fully that self-consciousness disappears. "Time flies when you are having fun!" The person is both fully engaged in the work being done and simultaneously possessed by a strong sense of awareness and inner peace. Flow is "the way people describe their state of mind when consciousness is harmoniously ordered, and they want to pursue whatever they are doing for its own sake."[6] This is very close to the manner in which Saint Thomas Aquinas de-

---

6. Mihaly Csikszentmihalyi, quoted in Katherine Wilson, "The Rhythm of Engagement," *Overland* 201 (Summer 2010) 14.

fined the virtue of *eutrapelia*: "And so there is a virtue in play which the Philosopher named *eutrapelia*. Someone is said to be *eutrapelos* or 'well oriented' because he is able to convert words or actions into relaxation."[7] Flow is close to the monastic way of living and working in mindfulness; ideally, the activity becomes transparent, wholly engaging yet allowing space for a parallel awareness. Part of the secret of monastic living is moving the emphasis from the objective productivity of what is done to the subjective dispositions in which it is done. For most new entrants this is a revolutionary change in attitude and in fixing priorities that requires patient mentoring and much good example.

All this seems to be practical common sense. But there is more to this situation than may be immediately apparent. Such a period of reorientation has a symbolic value. The necessity of learning and relearning marks newcomers as people who have a lot yet to acquire. It is an invitation to them to see themselves as disciples or apprentices in the school of the Lord's service. No matter how well they think they knew the community before entry, no matter how many other monasteries they may have visited, no matter how wide their reading of monastic literature, no matter what skills they have acquired in the course of life's experience, when they start their monastic life there is no other place to begin but at the beginning.

This was more obvious when I entered the monastery in 1960 than it is now. The lifestyle of a Cistercian monastery at that time was exotic, medieval, and austere. Entering it was like diving into cold water; the initial shock induced a kind of temporary numbness. Before long the novice had lost his clothes, his hair, his name, even his power of speech. Everything by which I had identified myself was set aside, and, meanwhile, a new identity was yet to be formed. We new novices existed in a kind of limbo. There were many elements in

---

7. *Summa Theologiæ* II-II, q. 168, a. 2; see also Hugo Rahner, *Man at Play; or, Did You Ever Practise Eutrapelia?* (London: Burns & Oates, 1964).

daily life that were incomprehensible. Some ritual quirks were taken very seriously; the seat was raised with the hand nearer the altar; on entering the choir stalls you rotated clockwise if you were on one side and counterclockwise on the other; if you entered the sanctuary, the right foot went first. And there were three kinds of bows that were not to be confused. Because everything was unfamiliar, instruction was necessary. This was accepted on both sides of the formation divide. We were "new chums," as they used to say in colonial Australia, and we had to be shown the ropes.

Today, when community lifestyles are closer to normality, the need for practical instruction is less apparent.[8] Yet, in most communities, there are hidden traps: invisible boundaries that newcomers cross at their peril, distances to be maintained, topics not spoken about, feathers to be left unruffled.[9] There is much to be learned, and there is still a need for some of the values of monastic life to be learned by doing.

In such a perspective the task of formation is seen as helping the trainee to act and feel as one of the community. This is done through instruction, supervision, approbation, and correction until the newcomer gets it right—whether it be a matter of bowing during the Office, setting up the refectory, or intoning a psalm. For those who emphasize this aspect of formation, the understanding is that "the life" will sort people out, and not very much attention is paid to inner experiences, except insofar as they interfere with the person's capacity to "live the life." The emphasis here is mainly on objective rather than subjective factors; yet it soon becomes evident that where

---

8. Perhaps there is scope to give greater emphasis to ritualizing the transition into monastic life with a view to reinforcing the perception that it is discontinuous with what went before. See Gerald A. Arbuckle, "Planning the Novitiate Process: Reflections of an Anthropologist," *Review for Religious* (July–August 1984) 532–46.

9. See Guire Cleary, SSF, "Challenges for Communities' New Members," *Review for Religious* 65.1 (2006) 30–42.

intractable obstacles to performance exist, more often than not the source of the difficulty is subjective and will be remedied only when these personal issues are appropriately addressed.

An important area in which training can occur is the asking and receiving of permissions. This is more than an exercise in enforcing the submission of those in formation. Ideally, it is practical training in discerning what is consistent with monastic beliefs and values. Sometimes an oracular response is sufficient: "Yes, it is appropriate that you go to your aunt's funeral," or "No, it is not appropriate for you to dispose of all your assets before profession." This may give rise to discussion or to private reflection, or it may simply be accepted as the final word. A fuller response might be, "The reason I say this is the following . . ." In this way the asking of permission becomes an occasion for a conversation that trains the person in applying abstract values to concrete situations.

Later on in a person's monastic development, it may be possible first to quiz the person on what values are operating in making the request and coming to a choice and then to help resolve any conflict between different values. A sign that the time of formation is coming to an end is when it is possible simply to offer accompaniment in the process of discernment and to affirm the other person in the conclusion reached. They have reached the point where they are able to discern for themselves what is right and good for them, and the only question is whether it is also right and good for others who are affected by the proposed course of action.

Monastic Education

Probably because it emerged from the medieval monastery, where monastic schoolboys made a seamless transition into the novitiate, formation used to be seen as a matter of teaching and learning, quite similar to what happened at school but with a different curriculum. This tendency was strengthened when male candidates passed quickly through a novitiate and proceeded to seminary-like studies for the priesthood. In more recent discussions among formators, it has become clear that in the mind of some the term "formation" continues to be regarded as virtually synonymous with "education." When formation is approached with such presuppositions, the same techniques are thought to be appropriate. "To speak and teach are appropriate for a master; to the disciple it belongs to be silent and listen" (RB 6.5). The communication of monastic tradition, however, requires an approach different from that of the schoolroom or lecture hall, one that we will explore in a later chapter.

Saint Benedict places a high priority on the abbot's role as teacher, and he demands skill in this area of all those who are appointed to positions of service in the community. What this means is that those who make the decisions and give the orders must be able to build up an environment of shared meaning that makes the prescribed actions reasonable. They should be able to communicate with the members of the community and express in words the values that are embodied in the decisions taken. For those in key positions in the monastery, it is not enough that they live the life; they must be able to explain it to others and to communicate its meaning.

One of the prime requirements of the period of monastic formation is to help newcomers appreciate and make their own the beliefs and values by which the community aspires to live. This transmission is effected by different means, formal and informal, individual and group, structured and heuristic. The important thing to remember is that it will not happen by accident or omission. Forethought, planning, and constant adaptation are necessary.

With the rediscovery of the value of systematic education for the nonordained monk and for nuns, we may ask what kind of studies will help in the stabilization of a monastic vocation. There is no doubt that a liberal education with its broadening of horizons can play an important role in allowing the monk or nun to deepen their understanding of the world in which they live. Many will have made some progress in this area before they entered the monastery. Some theology is essential. It seems to me, however, that the most important field of study is the monastic tradition, from its very beginnings until the present, including its history, culture, spirituality, and biography.[10]

Some monks and nuns will be attracted to pursuing monastic studies at an academic level, and this specialization is a great service to all monasteries. For most, however, it will be more a matter of learning to mine the centuries of tradition for a better appreciation of the beliefs and values by which they are called to live. If they are called to be professionally trained in other areas, this basic initiation into monastic sources will serve to give a distinctive seasoning to their area of specialization. At a time when monastic libraries have a wide variety of books on monasticism, when many lay people are interested in Benedictine spirituality, when most monks and nuns are better exposed to the tradition than ever before, it seems a shame that it can be difficult to persuade mature-aged monks and nuns to keep refreshing their acquaintance with the riches of their own tradition.[11]

As a novice I was surprised to be told that later in life I would find great spiritual nourishment in what Saint Benedict abashedly names "a little rule for beginners" (RB 73.8). Yet, as its final chapter hints, the Rule has the capacity to become a portal to a much wider world. It opens out into the large body of monastic and patristic literature both before and after the time of its own composition. This is a body of literature

---

10. It has to be said also that, although such study is greatly enhanced by a knowledge of the relevant languages not often present nowadays, there are available good translations and studies than can help newcomers make direct contact with the tradition fairly early.

11. See M. Casey, "Marketing Monastic Tradition within Monasteries," *Tjurunga* 60 (2001) 27–52; *An Unexciting Life: Reflections on Benedictine Spirituality* (Petersham, MA: St. Bede's Publications, 2005) 407–43.

that expresses and communicates the monastic culture that has grown up around the Rule in the past fifteen centuries. Delving into its depths gives us a perspective on monastic life that complements the conditioning that we have received from our participation in the social movements of the twentieth and twenty-first centuries. It can be a refreshingly new perspective on the issues that confront us on a daily basis.

Here I would like to suggest that the writings of the twelfth-century Cistercians can be of great profit even for those outside the Cistercian ranks. The monastic theology that was developed at that time is characterized by great insight into the way that monastic life interacts with human experience. In the best sense of the term it is a strongly subjective theology—that is to say, it is mostly concerned with the subject, the recipient of grace.

The monk's waking day, as envisaged in chapter 48 of the Rule, is divided among liturgy, work, and reading. This balance of activities is part of the genius of the Benedictine vision. The importance of this equilibrium was particularly emphasized by Aelred of Rievaulx, who wrote, "Let us flee from idleness by the variety of exercises . . . and thus we will protect our quiet by a change [*vicissitudo*] of occupations."[12] Abbot de Rancé was of the opinion that "a monk would not know how to use profitably the time remaining after other duties have been done without having recourse to spending time in manual work. There are fewer persons than one may think who can give themselves every day to seven or eight hours of reading."[13]

---

12. Aelred of Rievaulx, *De institutione inclusarum* 9; CCCM 1, 644; see Charles Dumont, "St Aelred: The Balanced Life of the Monk," *Monastic Studies* 1 (1963) 25–38. A fuller version is to be found at COCR 18 (1956) 177–89.

13. Armand-Jean de Rancé, *La Régle de saint Benoist nouvellement traduite et éxpliquée selon son veritable esprit*, vol. 2 (Paris: François Muguet and George & Louis Josse, 1689) 266–309.

Today even two or three hours spent in reading would be excessive for many, especially, one may conjecture, for those coming from a culture where adults spend about two hours a day on the Internet and watch three hours of television.[14] And younger people use electronic media even more. It is probably not alarmist to fear that we may be in danger of losing the capacity to enjoy the leisurely reading that monastic life has traditionally provided.

The goal of all monastic education is summed up in the title of Jean Leclercq's famous book, *The Love of Learning and the Desire for God*.[15] If, at the end of their period of formation, monks and nuns emerge with a love of reading, an appreciation of their own tradition, and an aptitude for ongoing study, a foundation is laid for a lifetime's profiting from the monastic patrimony. Initial formation ideally lays the foundation for ongoing or lifelong formation. A habit of good reading will sustain monks and nuns in many difficult passages of life and will prevent them from becoming intellectually stagnant. One who is content to be in a nook with a book (even an e-book) will find in reading a ready source of innocent enjoyment and a stabilizing refuge in times of mental or emotional confusion.

---

14. See Nicholas Carr, *The Shallows: What the Internet Is Doing to Our Brains* (New York: W. W. Norton & Company, 2010) 86–88.

15. London: SPCK, 1978.

Chapter Four

A SKILLED SENIOR

God is at work in the hearts of those who come to us, and meanwhile the community is shaping their monasticity through various channels. Monastic tradition and canon law provide that, in addition to these, a person or persons be designated with the specific duty of caring in an intensive way for new entrants, "who will diligently pay attention to them in everything," as Saint Benedict says. This goes beyond the tasks shared with other members of the community—inspiring, training, and educating newcomers. It means assuming the complex role of accompanier, counselor, mentor, supervisor. In many cases this will also involve "spiritual direction," whether or not it assumes that name.[1] In ordinary situations, however, the formator should not act as confessor for those under his authority.

Part of the difficulty formators often encounter in their task is its complexity, requiring different skills, some of which may seem contradictory. At different times they may be expected to be teachers, counselors, spiritual directors, group facilitators, work organizers, peacemakers, and masters of ceremonies. Often this is without much professional training or preparation in most of these areas. In addition, they have to cope with the ordinary challenges and inconsistencies of their own

---

1. In some places those in formation are encouraged to have a spiritual director distinct from their formator. I understand that this is designed to protect the person's freedom of conscience, and I appreciate that two persons acting complementarily can fill different roles, but I am not sure that this always proves to be a helpful division of labor. On the one hand, the possibility of playing one off against the other exists; on the other, each person in the helping role may neglect necessary challenges on the assumption that these are the responsibility of the other person.

lives and to deal with the negative forces that are sometimes unleashed by the work they are doing with newcomers.

Like the abbot, who is required by Saint Benedict to manifest both the harshness of a master and the affection of a father (RB 2.24), formators may find themselves conflicted about whether to insist on objective observance or to be patient and even indulgent toward someone who is experiencing severe subjective difficulties, giving them time to dig around and spread manure instead of chopping down the tree. If there is expressed or unspoken pressure from the superior or the community to cut short the process and demand immediate compliance, the dilemma is especially painful. "Harmonizing strength and tenderness surely constitutes one of the most difficult goals to attain and most delicate to maintain at the heart of spiritual accompaniment."[2] It is made more so by our unconscious preference for one mode of operation over the other, even when the data suggest that we switch approaches. "What we believe to be our personal gift in this area also risks becoming a particularly weak point."[3] To be noted, however, is that this dilemma or dialectic between comfort and challenge is not unique to formators or to monastic life. It is something that confronts all the churches.[4]

This is where it is helpful when the community as a whole takes responsibility for the general training of newcomers without, of course, intruding on matters more properly treated in the internal forum. Those with whom newcomers work, for example, should be encouraged to deal directly and sensitively with problems or issues that arise at work; a master of ceremonies should be the one to correct their rubrics; the

---

2. André Louf, *Grace Can Do More: Spiritual Accompaniment and Spiritual Growth* (Kalamazoo, MI: Cistercian Publications, 2002) 147.
3. Louf, *Grace Can Do More*, 148.
4. See Charles Y. Glock, Benjamin B. Ringer, and Earl R. Babbie, *To Comfort and to Challenge: A Dilemma of the Contemporary Church* (Berkeley: University of California Press, 1967).

refectorian should speak gently to them about any messiness in this particular area. In every case these minor officials are being proactive in easing the transition into the community life in a natural way, one less likely to cause unnecessary drama or humiliation.

When, because of shortage of personnel, a formator has to assume responsibility for everything that concerns the novices or juniors, there is danger of overexposure. The situation is even more serious when formators have other senior positions within the community. This results in the newcomer's experience of monastic life being funneled exclusively through a single person, one with many other concerns. That ever-present person is then perceived by those in formation as dominant and powerful, even though formators themselves commonly confess to an abiding sense of powerlessness. Wherever there is perceived power, resentment will arise, usually signaled by rebellion, passive aggression, or private mockery, but sometimes masked by supercompliance. In this way it becomes harder to build up a sound formative relationship. Where interaction is spread more broadly throughout the community, formators are freer to fulfill their essential role.

The specific task of formators is to establish a formative relationship with those for whom they are responsible. This relationship is based on the fact that the formator is officially charged to care for newcomers and so spends much time with them. When particular persons are appointed as formators, this becomes their major employment; they "are not to be burdened with other tasks" (can. 651.3, CIC). The relationship is all-important. In my experience, formators are constantly concerned about the quality of their interaction. Often they tread lightly lest an unexploded mine destroy any hope of building up or maintaining a solid fund of mutual trust. Like the abbot, formators need to relate to persons of different character and temperament, some of whom they may find impenetrable. It is necessary to adapt themselves and their tactics so that they may perform their essential service: winning souls by helping them to open themselves to the life-giving possibilities that monastic life provides.

Underneath this concern for maintaining good relationships there needs to be a degree of vigilance about one's own life. To be effective, formators have to learn to live in harmony with their own consciences. This means an integral living of the monastic life—for its own sake and not merely to impress those in their care. It is the formator's task to embody in action the beliefs and values that the community expects the newcomer to internalize. The task of modeling is significant because it is more than merely good example seen at short range. It is demonstrating that the way of life is livable, that it produces good results, and that the formators are practicing what they preach. There is often an unconscious process of imitation at work here. Occasionally, to the extent that there is a strong affective bond between the formator and the novice or junior, a subtle mimesis occurs in which the formator's personal style is in some way reproduced by the other. This might be the way of walking, or bowing, or reading in public, or the intonation given certain words. It is amusing to watch, but harmless. It gives ground for the hope that along with the exterior mannerisms some of the beliefs and values may have been transmitted.

The most important event of the formative relationship is the regular meeting in which everything can be discussed but in which the formator gradually steers the conversation away from the external world toward providing an opportunity to express how novices or juniors are experiencing the monastic way of life, how it is impacting on their sense of self, and what seems to be the movement of grace within their hearts. This will be treated in some detail in a later chapter.

Because nothing is excluded, issues are often raised in something of a jumble, with the risk that sudden urgencies may displace the steady exploration of a particular theme or concern. Dryness in prayer, anxiety about family members, interpersonal conflicts, a sudden onset of sexual temptation, concerns about health, loneliness, difficulties with studies, and many other sources of disturbance may interrupt the anticipated flow of conversation and demand attention. This requires much patience on the part of formators and a willingness to be detached from whatever agenda they had intended to pursue.

At the same time it needs to be recognized that sometimes these unexpected emergencies may be red herrings designed to move the conversation away from an area that is threatening. Too many sidetracking issues should be regarded with a degree of caution. The whole period of formation should not be consumed with extinguishing spot fires without ever having the opportunity to move deeper into the realms where the Spirit is at work. At some point the formator needs to draw attention to the omission and suggest that it might be time to remedy it. There is something else. The possibility needs to be considered that the formator is, in some subtle way, rewarding the other person for bringing problems to the fore, since dealing with problems can make the formator feel important. Good news or bad news must be received with equal inscrutability. Otherwise the whole truth will never be told.

Formators' interaction with those in their care is not limited to formal interviews. Getting to know others is more than listening to their self-descriptions. Living together means that casual observation of behavior and body language can provide a context for interpreting what persons say about themselves. Sometimes a chance remark made while sharing some mundane task provides a vital clue to the interior state of the novice or junior. Doing things together and being involved in little projects is, especially for males, a good opportunity for coming closer. Often, when it comes to practical tasks, older newcomers, arriving with skills honed during half a lifetime, will be better equipped to suggest how to proceed. The silliest thing to do in this situation is to stand on our dignity. This is the time to pay due respect to their prior learning and to allow them to use their gifts for the benefit of all. We do not form only by being assertive. Appropriate meekness often sends an important message that many honeyed words cannot convey.

Mindfulness of the work of the Holy Spirit relieves formators of the responsibility for solving every problem and pouring balm over every wound. Even if, unusually, there are no others in the community who can intervene creatively, we must have confidence that unintentional omissions, misjudgments, and mistakes will do no permanent damage. We cannot expect ourselves to be omniscient and omnipotent; those qualities belong to God. We do our best even though, at times, that seems little enough. It helps if we don't overinflate our expectations of what is possible. We may find some comfort in developing the gentle art of self-mockery, which can prevent us from being overcome by discouragement when the best laid plans go adrift.

At several meetings of formators I have asked whether any of them have been the targets of anger or aggression from those whom they are trying to help. In all of these sessions everyone present had sometimes been the object of rage, and two or three (both male and female) had been physically assaulted. It is all very well to say that it is healthy for novices and juniors to vent their anger, but its impact on the formator is considerable. Apart from the fact that being caught in a storm of rage is never pleasant, there are other insistent questions that disturb the formator's equanimity. Have I been guilty of a serious misjudgment or been remiss in my pastoral care? Have I completely misread this person? Is this the sign of some deeper, more serious problem that requires investigation? Will I be able to continue working with this person? Is this the beginning of the end? How can I remain calm while being assailed by so many accusations?

Another aspect of such situations is worth stating. Many of these formators expressed little confidence that in the event that these grievances or complaints were repeated to a superior, they would receive a fair hearing. Novices are sometimes deemed both more precious and more precarious than formators, and so it is considered more important to support them than to stand side by side with those who have been appointed to serve in the front line. It may be added that frequently these outbursts are occasioned by an attempt on the part of the formator to offer a correction or a challenge considered important for ongoing growth. Appealing to a higher authority is a way to deflect the challenge and avoid the need to change. If it works once, there is a strong possibility that it will be tried again.

It is important that the members of a community understand the challenges of the formators' task and support them not only in their work but personally. Too often formators become the butt of widespread criticism because of what they are perceived to do or not do in respect of some or many in their care. Without suggesting that all criticism is unjustified, because plainly it is not, I would say that it is important to trust the judgment of the person on the spot who has the most information about what is happening. For example, there are often good reasons of which the critics may be unaware for delaying a correction or for permitting exemptions from the rule. Also, when a novice or junior leaves, the reason behind the departure is not always public knowledge. The rules of confidentiality mean that a formator is not always able to counter a false report, whether it derives from the person involved or is used by somebody else as a ploy in domestic politics.

Self-care is essential so that formators make sure to replenish themselves physically and spiritually. Effectiveness in helping others requires a good level of serenity. This is attained only through self-knowledge and a warm self-acceptance. Especially in the beginning, it is important for formators to have some form of supervision to help them see how their work is affecting them and how to maintain their own sense of self while continually emptying themselves in order to serve others better. It would be interesting to find out the casualty rate among formators. How many have become discouraged and disillusioned? How many have burned out? How many have fallen into crisis? How many seem to have lost their own vocations? Of those who came to a sticky end, how many had access to supervision in their ministry?

And when all else fails, there is prayer. This is what Saint Benedict regards as the most potent means of pastoral care, even in the case of the severely recalcitrant. One of the important lessons to be learned from such an effective abbot as Saint Aelred of Rievaulx is the primacy to be given to prayer as a complement to the painful awareness of one's own inadequacies. In a general way, we take upon ourselves the burden of specific intercessory prayer for those for whom we are responsible. In times of special trouble, we enter into their troubles and ask for relief. We also pray for ourselves and bring our frustrations, limitations, and disappointments before the Lord. Sometimes we pray for guidance or courage or patience, but often it is just a matter of presenting ourselves to Christ in our reality, perhaps finding comfort in the fact that he also lost one out of the Twelve and that the others did not seem to be turning out so brilliantly, at least at first. Prayer allows us to reframe our experience as formators within the context of God's paradoxical dealing with humankind. We may not presume to interpose ourselves between God and others. We cannot insulate them from the challenges of monastic life or the *dura et aspera* with which the way to God is sprinkled. We cannot exempt them from the entering into the paschal paradox. All we can do is to accompany them, supporting them as best we can, by prayer and whatever else is possible for us.

Formation of Formators

If we accept the reality that every person who comes to the monastery is different and will, therefore, need a unique formation, then we will be able to appreciate that it is almost impossible to prepare a prospective formator for every single challenge to be met in fulfilling that demanding role. It is, as Saint Benedict remarks of the abbot, "a difficult and arduous task to govern souls" (RB 2.31), although sometimes it can be delightful.

To have oneself received a good formation is universally acknowledged as the best foundation for the task of forming others. In fact, everything that the formator has ever done or experienced feeds into the way that the formative task is approached. Formative "success" depends on interaction between two real people. The only way formators can have a positive influence on those in their care is for them to be themselves. There are, however, two qualifications to be made. The first concerns the fact that today's generation needs a formation different from that given in the past. Formators who simply hand on what was transmitted to them may overlook some important new areas that need attention. Second, what is to be done when those who are appointed formators did not themselves receive a good formation? This may have been due to lack of suitable personnel, to overwork, or to a community situation in which, for one reason or another, formation was not a priority. On what resources can an unformed formator draw to form the next generation?

It is here that I return to a theme that I have emphasized already. It is the community in all its organisms that forms newcomers—the superior, the seniors, the officials, and all the brothers or sisters. The task of the formator is to bring these different influences into a unity and to accompany newcomers as they struggle to make their own the life that is being transmitted to them. A formator who strives to form others in a manner of life that goes beyond what the community lives will almost always be frustrated. Novices or juniors may live according to these higher ideals while they are still under probation, but as soon as they escape into the community, their standards will slip. During the time of formation it is possible to insist on higher standards. Formators can educate newcomers beyond the common level and teach them to read Hebrew and sing polyphonic motets, to the wonderment of all. All such attainments can be achieved without the cooperation or even the comprehension of the rest of the community. Specific monastic formation, however, is a matter of encouraging and sustaining novices and juniors to open themselves and offer hospitality in their hearts to what the community has to give. If the community has much to give, the newcomers will be well formed. If, on the other hand, the community has lost its way, there is not so much that formators can do to remedy the situation. Improvement probably requires a change in leadership.

To appreciate the gift that is being offered in earthenware vessels, newcomers need to expand their horizons and not arrive at rapid judgments, the integrity of which is jeopardized by their limited monastic experience. The best way to bring about a broader vision is to expose newcomers to the warm and appealing wisdom of monastic tradition. Much is written about "Benedictine spirituality" today, and it has created a good market for itself among the laity. We do well if we help newcomers to appropriate this spirituality by increasing their familiarity and love for the texts of monastic tradition. To do this we need to have a solid level of intellectual and verbal aptitude. Without such skill we will be reduced to being enforcers of practice or merely frothy "motivators," unable to equip newcomers to stand firmly on their own two feet and calmly face the challenge of continuing growth.

Formators who consider themselves lifelong learners in the school of monastic tradition are much better placed "to draw forth from their treasures things both old and new" (RB 64.9). So vast is monastic tradition that not much more than a sampling can be attempted in the time available; the rest remains as a potential resource for the rest of their monastic lives. What the formator needs, in order to communicate a zest for tradition, is some basic knowledge, much (but not too much) enthusiasm, and the knack of building bridges between texts of the past and questions of the present.

For this some kind of formal preparation is most helpful. A formator does not need an academic acquaintance with monastic tradition (although this may be an asset) but something more like an amateur's enthusiasm that can convey an invitation to read more deeply and more widely. Monastic tradition can become a "great truth" around which all can gather and from which all can learn something new every day.[5] The study of monastic tradition reveals the underlying beliefs and values that are at the heart of the community's existence and lays the foundation for eventual practice. It also relieves the formator of the responsibility for being the source of all wisdom; the formators' task is, rather, to open the gate to the pasture and allow those in their care to graze until they are full.

There are other areas of a formator's task in which some preparation is probably necessary. Some training in these may be available through short courses or outside a monastic context. These other areas include acquiring skills of accompaniment and listening, some capacity for helping people in prayer, a knowledge and ease in discussing sexual issues, an ability to recognize pathologies and to know how to refer persons to appropriate professionals and to understand the significance of their reports.[6] It is crucial that formators have at least a basic understanding of the dangers of transference, countertransference, and codependency if they are to avoid attempting to have their own affective needs satisfied within

---

5. See Parker J. Palmer, *The Courage to Teach: Exploring the Inner Landscape of a Teacher's Life* (San Francisco: Jossey-Bass, 1998), especially chapter 4, "Knowing in Community: Joined by the Grace of Great Things," 89–113.

6. The following is a list of signs that there may be toxic residue from the early years of life: (1) ungrounded fears, (2) hidden hurts, (3) undue anxieties, (4) envies and jealousies, (5) grave insecurity, (6) chronic feelings of inadequacy, (7) disproportionate anger, (8) generalized resentment, (9) bitterness, (10) vindictiveness, (11) excessive guilt, and (12) deep shame manifested through low self-esteem and self-rejection. Note the adjectives. Mild forms of these symptoms are sometimes experienced by many without need for serious concern. It is the disproportion, intensity, frequency, or duration of the symptoms that indicates the person is better referred to a psychologist.

the formative relationship.⁷ Regular meetings with a supervisor can help in the attainment of a good level of critical self-awareness so that it becomes possible to translate raw experience into a source of wisdom.⁸ Gatherings of formators to update their skills and share their experiences are good sources of support and encouragement. Especially when an appointment as formator is sudden and the learning curve steep, there can be a tendency to overindulge in courses and programs without allowing time and space for personal appropriation. The end result is often indigestion.

The most effective force in the creation of a good formator is time. After years of making mistakes and learning from them, formators will become aware of the importance of standing back to allow God to act in the lives of those for whom they are responsible and, at the same time, the importance of drawing fully on the human resources of the community and beyond it to ensure that newcomers profit from the grace embedded in the way of life through years of unseen fidelity and fervor.

---

7. There is a worthwhile chapter on transference in Louf, *Grace Can Do More*, 67–74.

8. Here are the signs of critical self-awareness according to psychologist Br. Ronald Fogarty, FMS: (1) greater aliveness, alertness, responsiveness, concentration, (2) higher self-esteem, (3) higher respect for and openness to others, (4) clarity of speech, (5) respect for reality, (6) a certain intellectual and emotional autonomy, (7) ability to keep pace with dialogue and not be lost in personal thoughts, (8) habitual benevolence toward self and others, (9) proactive (or responsive) stance to events and people rather than a reactive stance, (10) active rather than passive attitude to life, (11) willingness to take appropriate risks and to try new ways of doing things, (12) readiness to acknowledge mistakes and misunderstandings, (13) being at ease with differences of opinion or style, (14) transparent honesty, (15) living in the here and now and not in the past, and (16) being able to acknowledge that one would prefer to do X while doing Y effectively and wholeheartedly.

Chapter Five

TODAY'S GENERATION

In the past, vocations were largely self-generating. Practicing Catholic families, systematic religious education, and the high visibility of priests and religious meant that young people were routinely confronted with the possibility of pursuing a religious vocation. Monastic life was less visible, but news of it still spread through published articles, books, appearances in the media, and by word of mouth. Furthermore, in many places there was a good deal of support and encouragement for vocations. Larger families were proud when one or two of their members decided to commit their lives in this way. As a result, those with spiritual leanings had a ready range of possibilities they could examine in order to find a form of life that would suit their aspirations.

The current situation is different. The former delivery system no longer operates. Almost nobody will enter monastic life as a matter of routine choice. Monasteries have to be more proactive in making themselves known and in propagating the values monastic life embodies. In many Western countries, having a sound Catholic upbringing and education is no longer a guarantee that the next generation will continue to practice the faith that sustained their parents, much less that they will be interested in considering a religious vocation. Many come to maturity without ever having glimpsed a religious, and they are much less likely to have visited a monastery. For those lacking the benefits of Catholic family and school, the image of monastic life will be drawn mainly from the caricatures peddled by the media and half-digested courses in medieval history. Monks and nuns will be readily perceived as exotic and irrelevant anachronisms on the margins of life, representing values no longer accepted by the bulk of the population. The fact that young people may have learned from the media to regard the institutional Church with suspicion further reduces the likelihood that "pursuing a career in the Church" will be seen as a feasible option.

For many, the possibility of vocation will arise only in connection with the experience of conversion, whether from practical heathenism, from non-Christian or non-Catholic religion, or from lapsed or latent Catholicism. It is as though, in the absence of human and social infrastructure, God needs to intervene directly at the level of experience.[1] Like Saint Paul, such persons are flung to the ground by a heavenly light and their lives are changed. Maybe the revolution is less dramatic: a steady accumulation of little insights and the growing intensity of secret dissatisfactions and desires, coupled with the secret satisfaction of pursuing a path different from that pursued by their nonpracticing parents. For such people, entering a monastery will demand substantial changes, not only in becoming part of a new community but also in modifying long-established patterns of behavior and in acquiring new beliefs and values to support a different way of living. Through no fault of their own, many have grown up unchurched; their contact with the sacramental world is

---

1. "The spirituality of the future will not be supported, or at any rate will be much less supported, by a sociologically Christian homogeneity of its situation; It will have to live much more clearly out of a solitary, immediate experience of God and his Spirit in the individual. . . . That is why the modern spirituality of the Christian involves courage for solitary decision contrary to public opinion. . . . It has already been pointed out that the Christian of the future will be a mystic or he will not exist at all. If by mysticism we mean, not singular parapsychological phenomena, but a genuine experience of God emerging from the very heart of our existence, this statement is very true and its truth and importance will become increasingly clearer in the spirituality of the future." Karl Rahner, "The Spirituality of the Church of the Future," in *Theological Investigations*, vol. 20, *Concern for the Church*, trans. Edward Quinn (London: Darton, Longman & Todd, 1981) 148–49.

tenuous, their moral standards may be quite different from ours, and their personal philosophies may seem, at first, to be unsupportive of lifelong commitment to monastic living.[2]

These young people, however, are no worse than we were. They also have spiritual ideals and desire to make the world a better place. The problem, as far as concerns recruitment, is that they do not associate these ambitions with involvement in ecclesiastical institutions. They have learned to make a distinction between "spirituality" and "religion." Those concerned with personal spiritual attainment do not think immediately of the parish community or the Church or a religious order. Their first thought may be with the disciplines and philosophies of East Asia: different types of yoga, Buddhism, Zen. Or they may be drawn into Pentecostal-type groups. Certainly they desire community and are often generous in trying to create it. Their ignorance of the breadth of Church life is such that it does not occur to them that communal living is at the heart of what they perceive as the arthritic religious institutions of a bygone age.

Those who remain active in the Church often practice a form of Catholicism that may seem alien to those who have lived through the disjunctions of recent decades. Sometimes we who may see ourselves as "keepers of the flame" need reminding that we are not the masters of monastic tradition but its stewards. Alert to the signs of the times, we may need to allow the aspirations of an oncoming generation to reshape the tradition so that it will be as life-giving for them as it was for us. This may call on us to review some of our practices and to loosen the grip of certain prejudices. Those who are impregnably conservative may find themselves in the same boat as those who cannot get beyond the progressive zeal of

---

2. I have described some of the operating cultural influences in "The Rule of Benedict and Inculturation: A Formation Perspective," *Tjurunga* 62 (2002) 25. This has been reprinted in *An Unexciting Life: Reflections on Benedictine Spirituality* (Petersham, MA: St. Bede's Publications, 2005) 456. See also Christian Smith with Patricia Snell, *Souls in Transition: The Religious and Spiritual Lives of Emerging Adults* (New York: Oxford University Press, 2009).

their youth—both extremes effectively locked out of dialogue by their obstinacy and defensiveness. The truth to which they are blind is that communities that receive new members must adapt themselves to the new generation just as surely as those who enter must adapt themselves to what they find. Resistance from either side is a deterrent to growth.

The New Generations

In monasteries, people of several generations live and work together. In discussing the differences among generations there are two hazards to avoid. The first is unconsciously to regard one's own generation as the default and, therefore, to regard the others as somewhat defective or strange. The second is to regard the generations as homogeneous and to draw sharp boundaries around them. This does not correspond to reality.[3]

In general, the bulk of monastic populations belong to the "Dutiful Generation" (1925–42) and the "Baby Boomers" (1943–60).[4] The numbers of "Generation X" (1961–82) who entered and persevered are low, and members of "Generation Y" (1980–2000), sometimes called "the Millennials," are still arriving. There is a noticeable thinness of middle-aged members in many communities, with many older persons (among whom I include myself) assigned to positions that would normally have been filled by persons of lesser antiquity. And there is sometimes a lot of multitasking.

It follows that someone entering a monastery is going to discover a generation gap. There will be incomprehension on

---

3. People of all generations have many values in common, although they may express them differently. See Jennifer Deal, *Retiring the Generation Gap: How Employees Young and Old Can Find Common Ground* (San Francisco: Jossey-Bass, 2007).

4. Both the names given and the dates assigned to the generations vary among authors. The division of generations and their characteristics vary from culture to culture, but one of the effects of globalization is that there is a tendency to convergence.

both sides, and there will be a risk that "the establishment" will simply regard many of the practices and expectations of its younger members as "unmonastic." This is why it is important that we understand the subculture from which new entrants come and that we who are already established in monastic living may take the initiative to build bridges between the generations in the hope of achieving some fusion of horizons.

This does not mean that we make fools of ourselves by embracing youth culture in all its rapidly changing embodiments. It means remaining ourselves but being open to conversation, appreciation, and understanding. At the same time, we should not be afraid to share what we have gathered in many years of living and in our experience of monastic life. As in so many human situations, the generation gap will not lead to conflict if, instead, it becomes an opportunity for dialogue.

Let us reflect on some general characteristics of Generation Y, those born since 1980. In general, they have few or no siblings and have always been treated as special, often growing up in a relatively sheltered and protective environment. Some of those who express an interest in monastic life will have been homeschooled. As a group they are high achievers, confident in their own abilities; they prefer to be seen as collaborators rather than employees. They have a history of having studied hard and behaved well. They are good team players; they accept conventional values and play by the rules. They expect others to recognize their quality: you do not choose them—they choose you. Dealing with Generation Y is inconceivable without considering its electronic gadgetry and the networking and information-gathering possibilities that it has opened up to them.[5]

---

5. On the challenges that this reliance poses, see Bishop Gabino Zavala, "Social Media: Friend or Foe, Google or Hornswoggle?" *Origins* 40.25 (25 November 2010) 392–94.

Though, at first sight, persons of this generation seem like ideal candidates for monastic life, there are still a few hurdles to surmount. They may find difficulty in coping with the uneventful reality of monastic life; adversity will be even harder for them to survive. They may find it hard to deal with formators or superiors who are Baby Boomers or who belong to Generation X. These they may regard as having "lost the plot." Millennials often stand for overt fidelity to the Church authorities—especially distant ones—and for many discarded practices of devotion. The most serious question to be asked about many of these generous young people concerns the formation of conscience. On the one hand, there is evidence of scrupulosity in some areas and, on the other, a certain moral insouciance that derives from a form of religious education in which any semblance of moral prescriptiveness was studiously avoided.

Those of Generation Y who enter monastic life have an idealized conception of what they will find. They expect a leadership that is nothing short of heroic, rooted in solid tradition and guaranteed by the Church and Magisterium. They require that the members of the community practice what they preach. They want strong structures that are effective in implementing the fundamental vision, though they also want a community to be somewhat open rather than being locked into a self-serving status quo. Their ideal is transparency in governance. They want good levels of honest communication, and in particular they want to be respected, fully informed, and listened to. They expect to find a common life that is committed, hospitable, affective, and joyful. Peer relationships are very important to them. Besides this, they bring a contemporary moral agenda derived from their own upbringing. They will be concerned for social justice and reject any discrimination based on age, gender, or class. They will want members of the community to be environmentally responsible, aware of their carbon footprint, and willing to recycle and to take trouble in order to avoid adding to the degradation of the planet—so many new commandments beyond the original ten!

For most communities, satisfying all these expectations would require radical reform, even if the idealism were tempered by an injection of practicality. We have to consider the possibility, however, that this litany of aspirations is a call to us to draw from our tradition those elements of lifestyle that the younger people value most. There have been many reforms in the history of monasticism, all of them summonses to clearer focus and greater fidelity. The reforms that got it right were usually found to be hugely attractive despite the increased austerity. Recruitment to their ranks was no problem. On the other hand, reformed communities often encountered criticism and opposition from the unreformed who were, perhaps, envious of their success. Monasticism, like the Church itself, is in a constant state of ongoing reformation: *ecclesia semper reformanda*. We may find guidance in our continuing task of renewal and reform in the minds and hearts of those who come to us, remembering that "the Lord often reveals what is better to the younger" (RB 2.3) and that sometimes those that come have been sent by the Lord for this very purpose (RB 61.4).

With regard to the transmission of monastic spirituality, it has to be admitted that, at least initially, many younger newcomers will find this dauntingly austere. If bridges are to be built, we need to appreciate the elements that have sustained their spiritual lives previously. We need to treat these with respect since these are the dispositions that have brought them to enter the monastery. Newcomers may need time before they are ready to graduate from them.

Spirituality

Among the characteristics to be found among fervent young people, such as those who are responsive to youth ministry and who attend World Youth Day, are the following. Obviously none of them is universal and some of them are a little antithetical, but all of them have some currency in the body of people under consideration:

1. *Marian Devotion* may include not only saying the rosary but also an interest in various Marian apparitions and in the practices associated with them.

2. *Eucharistic adoration, processions, and pilgrimages* are for many a corporate means of accessing the contemplative zones of Church life—times to be still, to be led to prayer, and to experience solidarity in faith.

3. *Charismatic involvement* may provide some with a style of religious involvement that is more attuned to popular culture; in addition, the high emotional content may be an antidote to the boredom normally associated with religious practice.

4. *The practice of meditation* is not uncommon, whether in a Christian context or as part of an Eastern approach to spirituality or simply as a pathway to inner peace. Some adjustment of practice may be necessary in a monastic context.

5. *Obedience to Church leadership*, particularly acceptance of papal authority and the level of devotion to Pope John Paul II, may surprise an older generation.

6. *Reverence and a sense of the sacred* may contrast with the more horizontal or incarnational approach embraced by many older persons as a balance to what they experienced in their youth. This is not mere conservatism; for those involved it is the discovery of a hidden treasure in traditional practice.[6]

7. *Sacrifice and renunciation* are important religious values for those who have grown up in a hedonistic and acquisitive culture; it may lead to giving away material possessions,

---

6. Andrew Hamilton, SJ, writes, "Individual confession, visits to churches, and rituals that encourage a sense of transcendence will retain a place, particularly for young adults who discover them afresh." "Forty Years Away," *Eureka Street* 12.8 (October 2002) 37.

fasting, and other penitential practices long abandoned by the ageing Aquarians of an older generation.

8. *Prescription*: for those who have grown up in an undisciplined environment, there is an insight into the damage caused by excessive self-will and a consequent desire to be guided and instructed in the ways of spiritual life. They may seek a certain (if selective) strictness. Purposeful and structured communities will be more attractive to such persons than groups that present themselves as laissez-faire. An emphasis on material observances may be on the way back.

9. *Enthusiasm for externals* is often evident among this group, as well as concern for rubrics in liturgy and a tendency to ritualism, zeal for the religious habit, and a general interest in the visible paraphernalia of the Catholic Church.

* * *

These tendencies are by no means universal and are not without their own hazards, especially when taken to extremes. It is important to note, however, that many of these values harmonize well with monastic life, even though the practices in which they are embedded may seem alien. Those who have the pastoral care of such people must not reject outright the spiritual exercises that have sustained them, even though they may challenge some of their own convictions. The most successful communities of the future will be those who not only continue the noble traditions of the monastic past but also incorporate into their *conversatio* the spiritual ferment of the present. This is how it has always been.[7]

People entering today are different from candidates of the past. This is not necessarily something to regret; it is simply a fact to be dealt with and a potential blessing. The changing

---

7. See Judith Sutera, OSB, "Vocations on a New Frontier," *Benedictines* 54.1 (2001) 14–21.

profile of candidates suggests that we need to become more accepting of the variety of individual histories, less likely to perpetuate repression of tendencies that deviate from the norm, and more confident in the power of monastic tradition to provide a life-giving pathway to a wider variety of people. The broader demographic spread makes it imperative that the formation process be of sufficient flexibility to accommodate different generations, cultures, personalities, and needs without becoming so diffuse that it loses its capacity to imprint on newcomers the specific character and charism of the community that receives them.

Areas Needing Special Attention

Respecting, understanding, and appreciating the spiritual life of those who come give us a better chance of offering a more effective monastic formation. The truth is that, despite their many admirable qualities, there are significant areas in need of specific attention in the early years of monastic experience. Some of these I will now attempt to discuss.[8] The formation to be given will need to come through various channels: through the attitudes, behavior, and example of the community, through the teaching of the superior and of others in the community, through personal interaction especially with formators, through counseling and direction, and through supervision. For some of these channels, a systematic education that covers both theory and practice will be required.

1. *Formation to Solitude*. Adam of Persigne wrote in praise of solitude, "You have learnt from experience that silence is most friendly to divine love."[9] This may not be immediately

---

8. I have written about the values operating in many of these areas in *Strangers to the City: Reflections on the Beliefs and Values of the Rule of Saint Benedict* (Brewster: Paraclete Press, 2005).
9. Adam of Persigne, *Letter* 9; SChr 66, 158.

self-evident to all. For a generation for whom instant and constant connectivity is a priority, spending time alone and apart is a disorienting state to endure and a difficult one to market. The symbol for separation from the world is no longer the enclosure wall but the switched-off cell phone. A community will need to have agreed on some guidelines about how electronic media are used during the time of formation and how personal networks are to be managed. Some postulants will arrive with their cell phone serving as a personal timepiece, an alarm clock, and their only record of contact details for family and friends. The idea of doing without it would almost be like losing a limb. Access to the Internet is no more exotic for this generation than looking out the window. Indeed, if they want to know what the weather will be like, they are more likely to turn to the Weather Channel than to open the curtains. It is important that solitude and separation from the world not be equated with blankness and emptiness but rather be positively identified with the range of activities for which people entered the monastery: genuine community, silence, *lectio divina*, meditation, prayer. When the time comes for newcomers to become actively involved in the community's works of hospitality and service, it is hoped that they will have been given the chance to view these activities as an expression of the monastic charism and not as an escape from it.

2. *Formation to the Common Life*. Many of those who come to us today will have grown up with few or no siblings. At home they probably had their own bedroom and private space and later, for those who are older, their own house or apartment where they could do as they wished, leave things where they desired, and come and go as they pleased. Fitting into a community with a fixed timetable, defined boundaries, and limited personal space will be for them something of a challenge. Furthermore, the sharing of facilities will demand a level of sensitivity to the preferences of others and tolerance of their oddities that they may not have previously experienced. Com-

mon meals, with their inevitably limited choices, may be a trial for them, especially if they had previously followed a high-principled dietary regimen of some kind. Scheduled hours of rising, especially if it is early rising, will be an abomination, particularly because it will mean curtailing their late-night activity. We have become accustomed to the common life and, over the years, have adapted to it. For those arriving in it from the world of today, it is like being on a different planet with its own set of esoteric customs and a language that, though it may seem to be the same, will sometimes be almost incomprehensible. They will need to learn the art of intergenerational, face-to-face communication, made all the more important by the probable reduction in the extent of their electronic contacts.

People who enter monasteries always do so on a wave of idealism; what they find when they arrive sometimes comes as an affront to those high expectations. This may be due either to the intrinsic unreality and unreasonableness of what they envisaged, or it may be due to an inaccurate assessment of their own resources.[10] One of the tasks of the formator will be to help them to become more realistic both about the community and about themselves.

3. *Formation to Manual Work.* Almost all monasteries require that those in initial formation be engaged in some form of

---

10. "Individuals enter a religious vocation with a conscious motivation which tends to idealize both themselves and the institution. Entrance is motivated more by personal ideals than by conscious personal attributes; furthermore, role concepts tend to correlate highly with the personal ideals. . . . People enter idealistically, and this idealism may be realistic if it stems from ideals which are consistent with the actual self, especially in its latent component; such consistencies dispose to self-transcendence and possibly to the action of supernatural grace. However, in more than a few people, it seems that entering idealism is quite unrealistic because of subconscious inconsistencies." Luigi M. Rulla, Franco Imoda, Joyce Ridick, *Psychological Structure and Vocation: A Study of the Motivations for Entering and Leaving the Religious Life* (Dublin: Villa Books, 1979) 77, 84–85.

physical work. This can be for the purpose of filling in the long hours of the day, grounding them and providing some balance to other more sedentary occupations, engaging in community tasks, serving the community's needs, or giving an opportunity to assess their aptitudes. Often they will need formation in this area, especially if they have rarely done manual work. They will need to learn how to give themselves quietly to an unexciting and perhaps repetitive task, how to work with others and to take instruction, how to be patient with the inefficient monastic way of getting things done, how to cope with the fact that the completion of tasks is less important than fidelity to the Liturgy of the Hours. They may be embarrassed by their lack of manual dexterity and hold back, or they may push themselves forward to assume management of a project. In any case, tendencies often manifest themselves at work that may remain long hidden in conversation. A canny formator will be alert to watch what happens.

4. *Formation to Stability.* The idea of lifelong stability is not one that will be familiar to those entering. They will not know many marriages that have lasted a lifetime, and often their own parents will have separated or divorced. Among their contemporaries many have chosen not to marry, and among those who did many were divorced. Growing up in a world of rapid change, they are acutely aware that nothing remains the same for very long, including themselves. They are honest enough not to want to make a commitment that they believe they are unlikely to keep.[11] Here the image that the community

---

11. "One reason for the failing marriage rate is that the rising generation of young Australians are [sic] characterised by a tendency to postpone commitments. Having grown up in a turbulent, unstable and unpredictable world, the pace of change has taught them to anticipate change and, indeed, to embrace change. They are the 'keep-your-options-open' generation; the generation who are prepared to wait and see; the 'hang-loose' generation. Whether they are talking about a sexual partner, a course of study, a job, a set of religious beliefs, a political philosophy, a musical genre or a commercial brand, members of the

projects of itself is very important. If it sees itself as fixed and unchanging, then it is unlikely to appeal to the new generation who will look for a group that uses its solid tradition as a springboard for a dynamic interaction with a changing world. The picture of stability that I often use is that of the surfboard rider. Stability need not mean lying still in a coffin. It is just the opposite. It involves much energy to stand on the surfboard while the waves roil and roll beneath; it requires maintaining a balance while everything around is moving. Stability means staying with the process until a point of decision is reached and avoiding terminating the dynamic of growth because of temporary setbacks. Saint Benedict was aware of this, asking of the postulant a promise (not a vow) of stability at the very beginning of the period of probation.

Stability is also threatened by another feature of contemporary life, what has been called "the instant-gratification syndrome." Those influenced by this find it difficult to persevere with anything that does not rapidly yield the desired results. Because monastic life is more like a marathon than a sprint, some specific formation is needed in the appreciation of long-term projects. It has to be said that in more contemplative communities, where the geographical stability of enclosure is added to the notion of perseverance, the challenge becomes even sharper and the need for formation greater.

5. *Formation to Quietness*. Silence will be an incomprehensible bugbear to many who enter, just another rule to be subverted where possible. They will often complain that it leads to that most dreaded state: boredom. It is not only the young

---

Options generation will typically say, 'This is great, but what else is there?' Such an attitude is not conducive to early marriage or, indeed, early parenthood—which is why the median age of the mother at the birth of her first child has gone up from the early-twenties to early-thirties in the past 25 years." Hugh Mackay, *Social Disengagement: A Breeding Ground for Fundamentalism*, Sixth Annual Manning Clark Lecture (3 March 2005).

but our whole culture that is progressively becoming addicted to entertainment, a modern form of "bread and circuses."[12] The question asked by Neil Postman in 1985 is still relevant: Are we amusing ourselves to death?[13] This preoccupation has been seen as an outcome of the "culture of death" that permeates Western society.[14] It is not healthy. Coming into a monastery that, for all its hustle and bustle, has substantial zones of silence will be a shock to the system. The danger is that the newcomer will try to conjure up entertainment out of the habitual humdrum of daily life. Often, when the initial shine goes out of monastic life, the "ordinary, obscure, and laborious" quality of daily life begins to pall, and the search for novelties begins. Formators need to be aware of this and, so, ready to prevent this inability to endure solitude and silence from transforming itself into the well-known monastic vice of *acedia*—the restless incapacity to commit oneself seriously to anything and, at the same time, engaging in any number of energy-dissipating activities. As William of Saint Thierry famously wrote, "It is ridiculous to take up idle pursuits in order to avoid idleness."[15] This is why most of those entering today will need an explicit formation so that they are able to make the most of the relative leisure that monastic life affords,

---

12. "What is the dominant mode of experience at the end of the twentieth century? How do people see things, and how do they expect to see things? The answer is simple. In every field, from business to politics to marketing to education, the dominant mode has become entertainment. . . . In other centuries human beings wanted to be saved, or improved, or freed, or educated. But in our century, they want to be entertained. The great fear is not of disease or death, but of boredom." Michael Crichton, *Timeline* (London: Arrow Books, 2000) 442–43. See also Mark Steyn, "The Entertainment State," *The New Criterion* 17.1 (September 1998) 24–29.

13. Neil Postman, *Amusing Ourselves to Death: Public Discourse in the Age of Show Business*, new ed. (New York: Penguin Books, 2005).

14. Michael Hanby, "The Culture of Death, the Ontology of Boredom, and the Resistance of Joy," *Communio* (Summer 2004) 184–85.

15. William of Saint Thierry, *Golden Epistle*, 82.

instead of "giving themselves to idleness and story-telling," as Saint Benedict warns (RB 48.18).

Sometimes it happens that because novices are relatively disengaged, they are assigned many different tasks. They become a kind of parallel work force, a flying squad sent to plug any gaps that occur. These various activities are sometimes designed to keep them busy and to prevent them from spending too much time thinking about themselves and brooding. They may be encouraged to engage in all sorts of initiatives that help them to be involved and interested. Sometimes, despite canon law (can. 660.2, CIC), such multitasking seems like a successful ploy for ensuring perseverance; all that it is doing, however, is preventing them from going deeper into themselves and developing the self-knowledge that is the only sound foundation for humility and for future monastic living. Formation to solitude and silence and an appreciation of the spiritual power of leisure are necessary for all who wish to make the transition from the contemporary world to the very different ambience of the monastery. Replacing appropriate solitude with "useful activity" prepares the way for later crises and possible disaster.

6. *Formation to* Lectio Divina *and Prayer.* Just because a newcomer is able to read does not mean that the traditional practice of *lectio divina* will come easily to him or her. A 2010 book takes as a theme the saying of Marshall McLuhan: "A new medium is never an addition to an old one, nor does it leave the old one in peace." Nicholas Carr, the author, studies the effect of the Internet not only on our reading habits but on the neural pathways in the brain.[16] He notes that for many users

---

16. Nicholas Carr, *The Shallows: What the Internet Is Doing to Our Brains* (New York: W. W. Norton & Company, 2010) 237. The quotation is from Marshall McLuhan's *Understanding Media: The Extensions of Man* (Corte Madera, CA: Gingko, 2003). A seeming contradiction of this maxim is found in Robert Darnton, "The Library: Three Jeremiads," *The New York Review of Books* 57.20 (23 December

of the Internet, the experience of reading books has changed radically as their brains have adapted to electronic media. Internet users show a growing intolerance with sustained developments of a theme and a tendency to be sidetracked as if following up hypertexts. He speaks of "the permanent state of distractedness that defines the online life."[17] The older meditative style of slowly moving forward under the guidance of an author has been undermined. Thinking back on ancient book usage, he writes:

> The reading of a sequence of printed pages was valuable not just for the knowledge readers acquired from the author's words but for the way those words set off intellectual vibrations within their own minds. In the quiet spaces opened up by the prolonged, undistracted reading of a book, people made their own associations, drew their own inferences and analogues, fostered their own ideas. They thought deeply as they read deeply.[18]

In order for this mode of reading, so typical of *lectio*, to become part of a person's life, instruction, training, and supervision are necessary. It is important that all concerned be alert to the difficulty and that a deliberate effort be made to confront it. As part of our initiation into *lectio*, some training in the art of close reading is helpful. This calls for a deep involvement with each word, phrase, and sentence of what is being read, with the intention of savoring every element and allowing the text to produce echoes in the heart. For this to happen we need to slow ourselves down and overcome our preference for speed-reading. A good means to this end, and one that has other benefits as well, is to train people to vocalize as they read, quietly allowing the text to penetrate awareness through a sec-

---

2010) 22: "If the history of books teaches anything, it is that one medium does not displace another, at least not in the short term."

17. Carr, *The Shallows*, 112.
18. Carr, *The Shallows*, 64–65.

ond channel. As an antidote to chronic restlessness in the face of sustained reading, it may be necessary to consider adopting the practice of having *lectio divina* in common. Initially, it may involve reading a text as a group, reflecting on it together, and providing opportunities for silent prayer. This could be seen as basic training in *lectio*. Alternatively, having several novices or juniors reading together at a prescribed time and place may serve as encouragement for them to stay quietly with the text and not to be jumping about either physically or intellectually.

Formation in deeper prayerfulness is an essential part of the early years of monastic life. All those who come to us will have prayed before they entered; it was this practice of prayer that guided and sustained them in their vocational quest. They have had some experience in prayer, but progress, when it happens, will be counterintuitive. Its clearest indication is when prayer becomes difficult or seems to disappear.[19] At such a time they will need guidance and some help to find their way to a simpler form of prayer. If their previous prayer was heavily devotional, great prudence is required in encouraging them to embark on the more austere monastic path; there is danger of their falling into a piety void that they may find difficult to handle.[20]

---

19. This dilemma is raised and answered at length by Saint Aelred of Rievaulx in *The Mirror of Charity* 2:17, 41. A novice wants to know why he seems to have lost the gift of devotion after his entry. This question provided an opportunity for Aelred to speak about the sobriety typical of monastic prayer.

20. "There is also the common unrest that is characteristic of persons abandoning old habits when this does not come from a personal, existential need that is experienced at depth, but which is imposed on them by the community in which they live. This is what happened in the sphere of the liturgy after the Council. To be sure, it is not the vocation of the Church to act as the conservator of ancient and outdated treasures but to try, first of all, to satisfy the Christian needs of the faithful. Meeting these needs has priority over saving from destruction the treasures of Gregorian culture. On the other hand, for older people who have lived the Catholic faith, these ancient treasures are not simply *cultural* treasures. *They are part of the fabric of their Christian life: they are, as it were, the living skin of their religious experience*, and not simply a garment that we can at any time take or leave, even sometimes regretfully. These are not simply religious forms of

7. *Formation to Frugality.* The idea of poverty is not exclusive to Franciscans; a certain detachment from material goods is a common quality among most spiritual movements and a usual goal in any effort at reform. It is true that Saint Benedict's Rule insists more on common ownership and due permissions than on deprivation, but he does not expect monks to have a high standard of living. This is an area where his followers have repeatedly failed and have often caused scandal.[21] Monks' clothes, for example, are to be whatever can be bought locally and cheaply (RB 55.7). Today those who enter will have spent their lives surrounded by abundance. We will probably have to encourage them to break the habit of consumerism; retail therapy is not an option in the monastery. It is not a question of forcing people to live in discomfort; it is more a matter of encouraging them to see the difference between what they need and what they want. It is forming them not to make their basic contentment dependent on an array of material objects.

As Saint Benedict suggests in the sixth step of humility, a person who is content with little will nearly always be content (RB 7.49). On the positive side, many newcomers will be intellectually gratified if they find that a monastery is not part of a throwaway culture, that it avoids waste, recycles, and saves energy, although they themselves may need some modification of behavior if they are to live these worthy ideals.

8. *Formation to Chastity.* It is likely, but by no means inevitable, that people entering monasteries today have a more extensive history of sexual activity than those entering forty

---

expression, but they are the particular forms in and through which their religious life has become what it is. Here there is no room for a *dualism* between what is inner and what is outer. A good number of such people inevitably feel as though they have been skinned alive, as though they have been stripped of their own flesh." Translated with emphases added from E. Schillebeeckx, "Zijn er crisiselementen in katholiek-kerkelijk Nederland?" *Katholiek Archief* 21 (1966) 347.

21. See, for example, Ulrich L. Lerner, *Enlightened Monks: The German Benedictines, 1740–1803* (Oxford: Oxford University Press, 2011).

years ago. This does not mean that they have no sexual morality; it is just that their ethical instincts have been applied in a different direction: safe sex, avoidance of unwanted pregnancies, avoidance of exploitation and violence. Although chastity and virginity have their advocates, the very concepts are dismissed as absurd by large sections of the mass media, and the conduct of "celebrities" is scarcely a source of good example. Since the 1968 promulgation of *Humanae Vitæ*, many Catholics have publicly distanced themselves from traditional Church teaching on morality, and many religious educators have been less than enthusiastic in their endorsement of it. The scandalous revelations about sexual abuse of minors in the Church have further undermined its credibility.

The people who enter monasteries may not be entirely typical of their generation, but it is unlikely that they have been uninfluenced by the prevailing philosophy. It will be an unusual progression through the various stages of initiation into monastic life that does not give rise to some sexual issues. Any formation program that has at heart the long-term welfare of persons will include a comprehensive treatment of the theory and practice of monastic chastity.[22] The aim is, as Saint Benedict notes, to bring them to the point where they "love chastity" (RB 4.64). Chastity is an integral component of monastic *conversatio*; it needs to be understood and practiced in an adult way and not merely be a false semblance of the virtue, created by fear and repression.[23] Above all, an authentic approach to chastity needs to accept the fact that as human beings we have genital needs, intimacy needs, and generative needs, so finding human fulfillment in a chaste life is something truly extraordinary. Because this is so, genuine chastity

---

22. "Celibate chastity is another area where education is needed." Seán D. Sammon, FMS, "Rekindling the Fire!," 7, at www.champagnat.org/shared/Scritti_Sean/SeanCartaChama_EN.pdf.

23. I have a short treatment of chastity in *Strangers to the City*, 52–75.

is impossible without a fervent life of prayer and devotion. Richard Sipe is trenchant on this point:

> In studying religious celibacy for thirty-five years I have never found one exception to this fundamental rule: Prayer is necessary to maintain the celibate process. A neglectful prayer life ensures failure of celibate integration. . . . No matter at what point in or out of the celibate process you find yourself, if you really want to be celibate, you can begin today by praying.[24]

It is very unlikely that celibate chastity will come about as a result of inattention. Although not everybody experiences its demands in equal measure and almost nobody is troubled by continuous temptation, we can take it for granted that it will be an issue for most people at some stage in life. For this reason alone it is important to lay a solid foundation of supportive beliefs and values in the hope that eventually these will contribute to a mature celibate chastity and a happy, fulfilled life.

9. *Formation to Truthfulness.* Many formators are puzzled by the fact that those in their care do not always seem to tell the whole truth. There are several reasons for this concealment. First, our media-shaped culture is characterized by discontinuity rather than by coherence.[25] Having fragmented the truth into bite-sized chunks, each episode or aspect can be viewed from a different angle. This is another aspect of the relativism against which both Pope John Paul II and Pope

---

24. A. W. Richard Sipe, *Celibacy: A Way of Loving, Living, and Serving* (Alexandria, NSW: E. J. Dwyer, 1996) 54.

25. "Contradiction . . . requires that statements and events be perceived as interrelated aspects of a continuous and coherent context. Disappear the context, or fragment it, and contradiction disappears. . . . The fundamental assumption of that world [of television] is not coherence but discontinuity." Postman, *Amusing Ourselves to Death*, 109–10.

Benedict XVI have spoken.[26] For those formed by postmodernism, truth is flexible. In addition, many feel that their life story is a personal possession that they can adapt and modify according to where they are situated at a particular moment. As in the *Soviet Encyclopedia*, events can be reinterpreted to mean whatever corresponds to present thinking; there is no permanent objectivity. Today I describe myself in one way to this person, tomorrow in another way to another person. Different truths for different situations. Yesterday's truth has passed its use-by date. Even when confronted by facts considered incontrovertible, postmoderns are liable to say coolly, "That is your interpretation," the implication being that there are other equally valid ways of understanding matters.

Second, those who come from a shame-based culture (as distinct from the more common guilt-based culture of the industrial West) will often not wish to answer direct questions until they know what answer is expected or likely to win approval. They want to please the questioner by their response. For as long as they remain unsure of what is the "right" answer, they will be reluctant to say anything. If pressed, they will so qualify their response with words like "sometimes," "maybe," and "perhaps" that they leave sufficient room for themselves to maneuver in accordance with the cues given by the questioner. In such cases, open questions are more likely to yield an honest response than direct and closed questions. It is often helpful to begin with the general and, slowly, perhaps over several sessions, to spiral in toward the particular. Every semblance of an interrogation needs to be avoided.

A third type of untruth comes about when people are desperately hiding a secret that they do not want to disclose. This may occur, for example, when a person absolutely does not

---

26. See *Veritatis Splendor* 32: "But in this way the inescapable claims of truth disappear, yielding their place to a criterion of sincerity, authenticity and 'being at peace with oneself,' so much so that some have come to adopt a radically subjectivistic conception of moral judgment."

want to discuss sexual orientation or the fact that a brother is in jail. Any topic that may have some conceivable bearing to these areas is subject to blanket defense measures. As a result, unclear answers become almost a reflex action, and language is used as a barrier rather than as a means of communication.

The people involved in these three kinds of untruth would certainly be insulted if they were called liars, and it is probably better not to make a moral judgment about their attitude to telling the truth or to tax them with the inconsistencies in their narratives. The formator needs to be aware of the possibility that the whole story is not being told right now and to have the intellectual athleticism to keep adjusting to the story as it unfolds. It may also be helpful to pay attention to body language, which often gives an indication of when a person is switching from memory to invention.[27]

Formators can forestall a tendency to untruthfulness by projecting a warm attitude of acceptance and affirmation. Such an attitude can take the form of avoiding any kind of adversarial stance, being nonjudgmental, not registering shock or rejection in their body language, showing themselves trustworthy, and guaranteeing absolute confidentiality. It is probably unwise, in most cases, to use autobiography with the intention of stimulating greater self-disclosure in the other; this tactic has been known to backfire.

10. *Formation to Faith.* We live in an age of aggressive atheism, and it is not unlikely that those entering monasteries have been affected by it. Despite the fact that they wish to dedicate

---

27. On this topic see Paul Ekman, *Telling Lies: Clues to Deceit in the Marketplace, Politics and Marriage*, new ed. (New York: W. W. Norton & Company, 2009). Ekman gives nine motives for lying (329–30): (1) to avoid being punished, (2) to obtain a reward not otherwise readily obtainable, (3) to protect another person from being punished, (4) to protect oneself from the threat of physical harm, (5) to win the admiration of others, (6) to get out of an awkward social situation, (7) to avoid embarrassment, (8) to maintain privacy, and (9) to exercise power over others by controlling information.

their lives to God, their knowledge of the faith may be tenuous. This is true not only of those who have been unchurched or tepid in their practice; it is also true, to some extent, of those who have had a full Catholic education and who have been involved in Church activities or even spent time in a religious order or seminary. For many, their view of the Church may well have been derived mainly from the mass media, and their attachment to a parish and their sacramental practice may have been slight. It is for deficiencies such as these that some communities have instituted a course of light theology before the novitiate begins, maybe using *The Catechism of the Catholic Church*. In addition, it has to be said that the formation of moral conscience must be a priority—not just in relationship to the natural law but in a specifically Christian and monastic sense.

We need to engage in building up a moral consciousness of what kind of behavior is required of the follower of Jesus Christ and of one who seeks to embrace monastic life. We can, for example, ask candidates what sort of life follows naturally from what they experienced at the moment of their conversion or vocation. This is important because, before entry, the formation of conscience may often have been sketchy and selective, perhaps due to timidity on the part of instructors. The fact that instances of scrupulosity (not always connected with obsessive-compulsive behavior) are reappearing after a long absence adds a certain urgency to this task. It must also be remembered that those who come to us are unlikely to have been unaffected by the general absence of the sense of sin to which Pope John Paul II often drew attention.[28]

---

28. For example, *Reconciliatio et Pænitentia*, 18. It is probably better to speak of the absence rather than the loss of a sense of sin. It can scarcely be thought that the widespread guilt and scrupulosity in preconciliar times, and the elaborate casuistry practiced to mitigate these, were conducive to a genuine sense of sin. Joachim Jeremias saw the besetting fault of the Pharisees as not taking sin seriously. This failure found expression in two notions: casuistry and merit. Casuistry makes

* * *

From these considerations it becomes clear that a massive work awaits those who would engage in monastic formation today, with a great many parallel tasks to be completed within a limited time span. It must be obvious that no formator or formation team could accomplish all this unless other agents were complementing their efforts. This is where the superior and the community have an essential role in creating a formative ambience in which the charism may be handed on to the next generation. Because of the attitudinal chasm between new entrants and the community, it is necessary that every member of the community be consciously and seriously involved in living the monastic *conversatio* in its integrity so that a critical mass is established that is able to generate new life. If a community really wants new members, then the key element must be a fervent and enthusiastic embrace of the lifestyle to which it is hoped that people will be attracted. Slick advertising, glossy brochures, and interactive websites will prove unavailing unless there is a reality behind the image: a community that is "joyful, down-to-earth, and committed" and members who are "clear and confident about their identity and hopeful about their future," to use the language of the 2009 CARA report.

---

gradations among sins and thereby emphasizes the avoidance of greater sins while practically ignoring the lesser and the least. Merits compensate for sins, thereby rendering their malice more tolerable. Joachim Jeremias, *New Testament Theology, Part One: The Proclamation of Jesus* (London: SCM Press, 1971) 147–48.

Chapter Six

ASSESSMENT OF CANDIDATES

Sometimes I remark to potential monastic candidates that it is a long way from the front door to the monastic cemetery. Mostly they understand that I am not talking about spatial distance—in our case it is only a few hundred meters—but about temporal distance. For many who cross the threshold it will entail a journey of forty, fifty, or sixty years. At least that is what I am hoping. I know, and we all know, that only a small proportion of those who enter upon this adventure will reach the desired goal of interment among the monastic dead. But we can always hope.

In his *Commentary on the First Book of Kings,* Saint Gregory the Great has some good advice concerning the necessity of prudence and discernment in the admission of candidates:

> To be noted is that almighty God, in predicting the right of the king, has given to religious superiors a model of formation. They have care over the way of the strictest *conversatio*, and they should not grant easy admittance to those newly coming. Hence the excellent master of this strictest life and the learned disciple of supreme Truth have taught, "Test their spirits to see if they are of God," and "Let all the hard and rough things be told them so that they know to what they enter." So that the weak do not easily approach the way of virtue, let strong superiors never easily receive them. Rapid conversion often arises from precipitate reasoning, not from an increase of devotion. When the weak promise strong things, it is not the result of strength of soul but of confused discernment. Such as these the sage warned, "Do not lift a burden on yourself." Those who are in charge of others in the strong choice of regular life ought to receive

these converts to that life with discernment, since it is useful for them to know in advance whether the petition of those who come is the result of the soul's virtue or of the will's rashness. For those who are easy in their actions often urgently desire the roughness of the spiritual life so that it may seem that what they seek comes from great virtue of soul.[1]

During the decades that follow entry there will be many changes and reversals of fortune as monastic life begins to shape the spiritual physiognomy of those who embrace it. What is to be desired is that the ongoing process of formation has a certain consistency or stability about it so that it delivers a single message and dissipates as little energy as possible through directionless initiatives.

There are many different moments in the community's interaction with those who wish to enter into its life. For candidates to apply, it is necessary that they know what is the nature of the monastic vocation and, more importantly, what kind of people are able to find life by following this calling. This means that we have to allow those interested to see what we are, who we are, and what we do all day. It is important that there be continuity in our self-presentation so that we do not present one image to the potential candidate, something entirely different to one who enters, and yet another later on. There have been cases of congregations marketing themselves as contemplatives-in-action where this description bears no relationship to the way the group actually operates. No wonder some feel they have been misled or even deceived when they discover the reality. In addition, as candidates pass through the various stages of monastic initiation, something like "synchromesh" needs to operate so that transitions are smooth and newcomers are not bewildered by the changing expectations that they are required to meet. Aids of different

---

1. Gregory the Great, *Commentary on the First Book of Kings*, 4:70; CChr 144, 330; SChr 432, 422–24.

kinds need to be in place so that novices can go from first to second and third gear, so to speak, without always having to return to neutral.

Attraction

I am often surprised by the easy assumption made by monastic communities that they are well-known and well regarded. It may be true that they are appreciated and highly esteemed by those who know them, but it may also be true that this circle of acquaintance is relatively small and does not include those elements of the population in which potential monastic vocations are most likely to be found. Outside the number of their friends (in the real world), those enlisted through social-networking sites, and those who receive their newsletters and Christmas cards, they may well be the objects of ignorance, indifference, or even mild hostility. Generating more information among those already acquainted with monastic life is unlikely to have much impact on vocations. Any attempt to promote a greater vocational awareness needs to give most attention to those likely to be accepted in the event that they eventually apply.

I am beginning to believe quite firmly that some people are born with a monastic vocation—in the sense that there is a deep sense of being called that predates any conscious decisions they make about the ordering of their lives. It may take years and even decades before they are prepared to recognize and name the nascent yearnings they experience, and then more time may elapse as they look around for a form of life in which such desires can be incarnated. Most often they do not know immediately what they want, although they may be relatively certain about which forms of life do *not* correspond to their deepest aspirations. They become long-term and often secret seekers. To the extent that this perception is accurate, recruitment must be seen less as a matter of creating a desire for monastic life in people than of providing information that will enable potential aspirants to identify the monastery as the place of their dreams. Commercial advertising strives to create or intensify needs in order to satisfy them. The work of vocation promotion is not about marketing monasticism as a desirable lifestyle but about allowing ourselves to be seen as we are by a target constituency—that is, by those who are looking for something that they cannot describe until they see it.

Making contact with potential candidates means reaching out to them where they are through effective channels of communication, especially the Internet. Tame advertisements in diocesan news media may achieve little. Pamphlets designed to accumulate dust in church porches may do nothing more than that. All our dealing with those who come to us must be characterized by a profound respect for the journeys that have led inquirers this far and for the integrity that has sustained them in their search. This means going out to them where they are—morally, intellectually, emotionally—rather than expecting them to be able to find us where we are. This demands of us a certain detachment, together with the recognition that those who come today will be different from the candidates of the past. This has one particular consequence: we must become aware of our own unconscious prejudices and seek to neutralize them, otherwise we may be looking for new life in places where it is not to be found and bypassing many real opportunities for recruitment.

When we think of an ideal candidate for monastic life, whether it be a self-portrait or its opposite, to some degree we tend to regard those who do not conform to that ideal as unsuitable. It cannot be said frequently enough: those who are interested in monastic life today are different from those who presented themselves a half century ago. Unless we have moved with the times, everything about such potential candidates will scream unsuitability. But, in a sense, it is *our* unsuitability to receive them that is the problem, more than any qualities or lack of qualities in them—our inability to accept them as they are and to give them the formation that will lead them to the richer and fuller Christian life that monastic life facilitates.

To repeat myself on this crucial point: people entering today are different from candidates of the past. This is not necessarily something to regret; it is simply a fact to be dealt with and a potential blessing. The changing profile of candidates suggests that we need to become more accepting of the variety of individual histories, less likely to perpetuate repression of tendencies that deviate from the norm, and more confident in the power of monastic tradition to provide a life-giving pathway to a wider variety of people. The broader demographic spread makes it imperative that formation processes be of sufficient flexibility to accommodate different generations, cultures, personalities, and needs without becoming so diffuse that they lose their capacity to imprint on newcomers the specific character and charism of the community that receives them.

We cannot afford to remain passive if we are zealous for the future of monastic life. In the first place, a study of monastic history is instructive. We soon find that the greatest recruitment booms occurred in reformed monasteries—that is, in those communities that responded appropriately to the signs of the times. Our first task in attracting vocations is to make of our communities the sort of places that potential candidates would want to join. This does not mean raising our standard of living until it no longer makes demands, but having clear ideals and practical strategies to convert these ideals into reality. Beyond this, we need also to consider what needs to be done if we are to attain an appropriate level of visibility in the Church. Mostly this means finding media and a language with which to communicate with our potential pool of candidates, although sometimes this may involve certain changes for ourselves.

We need to be clear about what we are doing when we invest in projects designed to increase our public visibility. There is a difference between public relations—especially when conjoined with fundraising—and recruitment. A cynic might say that an exercise in public relations almost always presents the community in its best light, spinning reality so that it accords with the expectations of those it is aiming to impress. Material intended to generate vocational interest, on the other hand, needs to be scrupulously honest and low-key, not hiding the *dura et aspera* but appealing to the generosity of those considering the matter. Inducing persons to enter a monastery under false or exaggerated pretenses will result in their becoming dissatisfied and eventually leaving—but not after much effort on the part of formators, expense, and, sometimes, drama. Inquirers must be encouraged to shed any romantic notions that might induce them to view monastic life through rose-colored spectacles.

First of all, we need to have a unified and corporate vision of our life that is clearly discernible in the way we live. We cannot tout ourselves as practitioners of poverty and simultaneously embrace luxuries reserved to the rich. We cannot preach prayer and live practically prayerless lives. To offer ourselves to candidates involves exposing our own lives to scrutiny. A fervent community is much more likely to continue attracting than one that is lukewarm or inconsistent. Those dealing with newcomers notice that it is the contrary practices of some members of the community that consistently generate the most negative responses.

Second, we need to make use of whatever human resources we have to make ourselves known. Real people speak more convincingly than glossy fictions. Most communities need to be convinced that vocation promotion is the responsibility of all, to be exercised according to the opportunities that are available to each. Only a few will be involved in assessment and discernment of candidates, but all should keep the issue of vocations in their hearts and in their prayers; they should be welcoming to those who approach the community as inquirers, as well as willing to share their own vocational stories when occasion offers and to present to the outside world a face that is honestly serene and happy in the monastic life. In addition, they should not be afraid to take the initiative and to invite persons they consider suitable to consider a monastic vocation—this simple action often serves as a significant starter of a fruitful process of reflection.[2]

Third, there will be practical questions that will need community backing, such as the extent of advertising, the media to be utilized, the image to be projected, the amount of money to be spent. How a necessarily limited budget is employed may best be resolved by building up a panel of outside advisers who can provide the expertise that will almost certainly be lacking in the community. Mistargeted propaganda is always a waste of time and resources.

Fourth, those dealing directly with inquirers will need to appreciate the merit of prompt responses, the importance of maintaining contact, and the necessity of being proactive in making suggestions about further communication. Many inquirers are timid about making contact, and failure to respond to a tentative approach will often result in their losing heart—at least for the time being. In the early stages it is probably prudent to avoid questions that may be perceived as intrusive. More can be gained by encouraging persons to understand their vocational attraction more deeply and comprehensively and to reflect on its consequences. Only then does the necessary question of what this attraction may ask of them seem less threatening. Vocation promotion is distinct from assessment and discernment; first, interest must be aroused and sustained; only then is there question of determining its quality and source.

Fifth, in singing the praises of monastic life it is important that its high ideals be clearly stated. There is, however, a dan-

---

2. "A personal invitation on the part of a brother is the single most often mentioned factor that has caused a young person, as well as those further along in years, to take a serious look at our life and ministry." Seán D. Sammon, FMS, "Rekindling the Fire!," 10, at www.champagnat.org/shared/Scritti_Sean/SeanCartaChama_EN.pdf.

ger here. We know that among the younger generations there is often a curious tension between high ideals and low self-image, which causes a certain amount of pain and can lead to indecision. We have to be careful lest we present an ideal so lofty that it seems practically unattainable. The monastery is a school of the Lord's service, as Saint Benedict notes (RB Prol. 45); in it we *learn* to make the journey from what we are now to what God would have us become. Our information releases must emphasize the monastic dynamic by which an imperfect human being is progressively transformed, by the monastic way of life and by God's grace, to become holy; it is not personal effort or prior innocence that is the determining factor, but humble perseverance in submitting to the purifying action of the Holy Spirit.

Sixth, it has been found that many vocational inquirers are most interested in hearing the stories of those who have already travelled a particular path. In the first place, they are inspired by the saints for whom religious life was the means by which they attained holiness. Beyond that they are prepared to be stimulated and encouraged by hearing of others who have made the journey from mediocrity or worse to a stable enthusiasm for spiritual reality. Think of how many vocations have followed from reading Thomas Merton's *Seven Storey Mountain*. Our history may not be as dramatic or as well told, but when shared it still has the capacity to move others—to provide them with the energy to take the next step. Those who monitor website visits have noted that sites that provide autobiographical accounts of religious vocations nearly always attract the most attention. Good example is always life-giving, and nowhere more than in a world where celebrity misbehavior is part of the staple diet of popular culture.

The community that develops a culture of vocation promotion is far more likely to be blessed with numerous inquiries than one that passively waits for expressions of interest. From those who present themselves, a selection must be made on the basis of their suitability for the way of life as it is lived in a particular monastery and of their degree of readiness to cross its threshold.

Let us now examine some of the elements involved in this further stage of the incorporation process.

Assessment

There are two distinct areas that must be discussed with inquirers as their vocation journey unfolds. The first concerns their generic *suitability* for the monastic way of life. Is the person likely to follow the community lifestyle without unnecessary hardship, difficulty, or distress? Persons not suitable may include those with a serious addiction, those whose psychological problems are such that their therapy demands priority above everything else, those too old or too young, those with civil obligations to be met, those who are too sick or feeble to live the common life. There is also the question of moral suitability. In the abstract, about 25 percent of the unmarried Catholic population is probably suitable, presupposing a desire to embrace monastic life. But only the combination of freedom from impediments with an active desire to pursue monastic life becomes a vocational indicator.

In judging the authenticity of a desire for monastic life, the first task we need to do is assess a person's suitability or potential suitability to embrace monastic observance for a lifetime. This assessment will be largely a matter of a judgment made on the basis of experience. Unsuitability definitely excludes; suitability joined with a sense of vocation is not final—it leads to the next step.

In those who are suitable we look for *readiness*. Among those who are suitable and who wish to enter a monastery, not all are ready right now to take the practical steps that would allow them to make the transition. Maybe they would profit from more maturity, wider experience, a longer period of acquaintance with the monastery. Maybe they need to finish a degree, to care for an aged parent, to pay off their debts, or to recover fully from a bout of glandular fever. In such a case the question arises about how to keep them interested while waiting for their degree of readiness to attain critical mass.

Parallel to the process of assessment is the more spiritual task of discernment. If assessment is largely a matter of data gathering about a person's life and comparison with an implicit profile, discernment is more concerned with coming to an understanding of the spiritual journey that has led to an interest in monasticism. Here the greatest enemy is speed.[3] The interior story will likely unfold in ever-widening circles, and what we look for, above all, is coherence. This is not to say that there will be perfect continuity in the narrative, but even where discontinuities exist, there will be a sense, when the call is genuine, that all things have worked together unto good. It is important to distinguish the prompting of the Holy Spirit from the movements of self-will. Sometimes those who push too hard are more engaged in following their own blueprint than in responding to God's call in the depths of their being. Often it may be necessary to remove the romantic vesture in which the aspiration is clothed in order to uncover the underlying reality.

No one in the business of vocational discernment claims infallibility. We simply do the best we can for everyone concerned. There are several lists of qualities that are usually sought in prospective candidates.[4] Nearly all of these inven-

---

3. See M. Casey, "Diagnosis and Discernment: *Ut Sapiens Medicus*," *Tjurunga* 74 (2008) 91–96.

4. Catholic Vocations Ministry Australia has circulated "Benchmarks for Applicants to Priesthood and Religious Life." This contains twenty-five items under three headings: "Human Development," "Christian Maturity," and "Identity with the Charism." Fr. Raymond Carey, a behavioral psychologist with a special interest in vocational discernment, approaches the matter in terms of the acquisition of requisite skills. See "Psychosexuality and the Development of Celibacy Skills," distributed at his workshops. See also Matthew Leavey, John Klassen, Paul Schwietz, Robin Pierzina, and Robert Pierson, "Qualities and Skills for Monastic

tories will help us to become sensitive to the issues concerned, though none of them is going to replace our immediate role in coming to a practical judgment. We can study lists of requirements and consult all the appropriate experts, but ultimately the decision belongs to the admitting superior, based on input from many different sources. Perhaps it will be helpful to review some of the areas in which more careful assessment is necessary.

Particular Points

The fundamental question to be posed about those who seek admittance is about whether they will fit in with the existing community and its way of life to the extent necessary for formation to take place and for sufficient ease of relationship to exist on both sides so that ongoing cohabitation is feasible. Miracles of mutual adaptation are possible but not frequent. Most cases are not so clear. All we can do is try to judge the likely success of the formation process on the basis of statistical probabilities and the everyday observations of those who have some knowledge of the candidate. Vocation directors have often accompanied potential candidates over a prolonged period, have listened to their stories, and, perhaps, have been the witness of their struggles. The deep understanding this relationship has generated is a valuable resource in making a final assessment. In addition, those nominated to serve as referees should be encouraged to speak frankly about the candidate on the understanding that this is in the candidate's best interest.

Fifty years ago, an entrant into my own monastery would have been a practicing Catholic with a Catholic education and, preferably, active in Catholic organizations. He would have

---

Life: One Approach," *Benedictines* 54.1 (2001) 6–13. Fr. James Palmigiano of Saint Joseph's Cistercian Abbey (Spencer, MA) has adapted this for his own monastery in "Qualities and Skills for a Candidate."

been of Anglo-Celtic background, aged eighteen to twenty-five, sober, presumed heterosexual, never married, chaste and possibly virginal, of robust health, with no psychological problems. He would have had a moderate education and showed himself stable in employment, with no criminal record. He would have been a good team player but with a capacity for solitude and prayer. He would have come from a "good Catholic family" in which the parents had remained together, and he would have good relations with several worthy siblings.

Occasionally, a present-day inquirer will conform to the profile of the past, but in most places the situation has changed, and it may be that many of those who find acceptance today would have been considered unsuitable in previous times. Because the world has changed so much, this means that the formation that we will give to those who enter will need to be different in many respects from what we ourselves may have received.

1. We can no longer assume that all who enter will come from a single *ethnic or cultural background*. Thanks to the Internet, potential aspirants shop around so that monasticism is becoming globalized, with persons choosing to enter monasteries far from their place of origin—even when monastic life is available nearby. In assessing vocations, one needs to be realistic in recognizing that radical changes in diet, climate, language, and culture can increase the degree of difficulty experienced by those making the transition into monastic life and, at the same time, having to respond to the particular demands of the formation process.[5]

---

5. See Gerald A. Arbuckle, "Multiculturalism, Internationality and Religious Life," *Review for Religious* 54.3 (1995) 326–38. M. Casey, "The Rule of Saint Benedict and Inculturation: A Formation Perspective," *Tjurunga* 62 (2002) 15–46; reprinted in *An Unexciting Life: Reflections on Benedictine Spirituality* (Petersham, MA: St. Bede's Publications, 2005) 449–90.

2. Some applicants may be *too young*. Recent work on the brain has revealed that the neural pathways, by which the frontal cortex exercises its controlling functions over the rest of the brain, develop slowly to reach their full effectiveness sometime between the ages of eighteen and thirty. "Fully functional frontal lobes are the prerequisite for social maturity."[6] From their operation comes the capacity for foresight, planning, impulse control, and empathy, and consequently they are vital for the quality of any life-determining decision. Maturity comes to different people at different times, and so it is important to look beyond chronological age to determine a younger person's suitability. Evidence of effective adult choices in all areas of life is the best indicator that a character has matured sufficiently to make monastic life feasible.

3. Some applicants may be *too old*. Many religious communities have an upper-age limit on potential candidates. Again, I have found that there is much individual variation. People are living longer, and someone who takes early retirement at fifty-five may have twenty years of life remaining or more. In some East Asian traditions it is considered normal for a man

---

6. This paragraph is dependent on Elkhonon Goldberg, *The Wisdom Paradox: How Your Mind Can Grow Stronger as Your Brain Grows Older* (New York: Gotham Books, 2005) 176–77. Goldberg is a clinical professor of neurology at New York University School of Medicine. For a comprehensible discussion of the new science of the teenage brain, see David Dobbs, "Beautiful Brains," *National Geographic* 220.4 (October 2011), 36–59. The stage of first full maturity is well delineated by Thomas Hardy in the first chapter of *Far from the Madding Crowd* (1874; repr., London: Penguin Books, 2003) 4: "He [Gabriel Oak] had just reached the time of life at which 'young' is ceasing to be the prefix of 'man' in speaking of one. He was at the brightest period of masculine growth, for his intellect and his emotions were clearly separated; he had passed the time during which the influence of youth indiscriminately mingles them in the character of impulse, and he had not yet arrived at the stage wherein they became united again, in the character of prejudice, by the influence of a wife and family. In short, he was twenty-eight, and a bachelor."

to become a monk after having pursued a career and raised a family; monkhood is seen as the crowning achievement of a successful life.

There are three potential reservations to bear in mind in considering the possibility of older candidates. The first is the simple question of physical health and energy levels. Monastic living is more challenging than it appears from the outside. Its relentless regularity, its structural constraints, and its comparative lack of opportunities for entertainment can surprise some who have for years relied on harmless hobbies and casual relaxations for their sense of well-being. The second is the danger of nesting—someone seeking a secure and tranquil environment that will provide for all their needs without too much being asked of them. In this case the considerable exertion required to throw oneself wholeheartedly into a completely alien lifestyle is often underestimated. Furthermore, nobody is excused from spiritual warfare in the monastery, and sometimes the appetite for this diminishes with age. The third difficulty is that, even with the best will in the world, each year after forty makes it harder for most people to respond creatively to the monastic formation process. This means that although it is easy enough to learn to do what everyone else does, it is much harder to internalize the beliefs and values that are meant to animate such behavior. In some cases, despite years of good living, much of the inner journey to self-knowledge remains to be completed.

4. The question of *sexual orientation* arises regularly in meetings of monastic formators. Recent Vatican pronouncements about excluding those with "deep-seated" homosexual tendencies from advancing to the priesthood are indicative of the concern many feel about this matter. Here, as in so many other areas, persons are best understood in the context of their individuality. As a particular community seeks to clarify its stance on this issue, there are at least these five areas to be considered.

i. It is understood that chastity is an integral part of the monastic *conversatio*. This principle cannot be compromised. In all probability the homosexual candidate, like the heterosexual, will need to have lived chastely for some time before entry becomes feasible.

ii. There are different degrees of same-sex attraction in terms of exclusiveness, intensity, and frequency of practice. A particular episode or series of episodes may need to be interpreted within a developmental context. A temporary or transitional phase of same-sex attraction or behavior need not necessarily be an indication of a "deep-seated" tendency.

iii. Candidates should not be implicitly encouraged to repress the awareness of their sexual orientation—a kind of "don't ask, don't tell" policy. Latent homosexuality continues invisibly to influence choices and can thus lead to situations for which the persons involved are unprepared and of which the true dynamics are not fully recognized by the participants or by those who seek to help them.

iv. In some cases, same-sex attraction is a threat less to chastity than to the formation of healthy and mature community relationships. Where it leads to extremes of attachment and/or detachment from certain other members of the community, it can disrupt the normal flow of everyday friendliness on which community harmony depends.

v. It is probably not helpful for members of a religious or monastic community to take sexual orientation as their primary identifier, for example by becoming defenders or propagators of gay culture, or members of an in-group based on sexual orientation.[7]

---

7. "Any brother who makes his sexual orientation central to his public identity would be mistaking who he most deeply is. He would be stopping on the roadside when he is called to walk to Jerusalem. What is fundamental is that we can love and so are children of God, not to whom we are sexually attracted. But it does not only concern an individual's personal sense of identity. We have an identity as

5. With the changing fortunes of marriage in many contemporary societies, *marital status* is not an issue for which universal norms can be set. Since candidates are older, many will have been in de facto relationships that have ended either by mutual consent or acrimoniously. Others may have entered marriages that have not lasted and have been terminated by divorce, legal separation, annulment, or by the death of the partner. Those responsible for admission will need to be familiar with the specific requirements of canon law in such cases. Dependent children must be taken into consideration. In most cases, entry into religious life is more than a matter of determining the freedom of the candidate to do so. A certain amount of emotional baggage will have resulted from the experience, and this will need to be explored and its ongoing impact assessed. All too often the intrapersonal dynamics that contributed to the failure of previous relationships can, at a later stage, pose problems for continuance in religious life.

6. The integrity of monastic life includes a lifelong commitment to *chastity*. This does not necessarily mean that perfect chastity or even continence is already achieved before entry. It is to be expected that the candidate will have had the experience of living without sex for a sufficient period of time to establish its possibility, to acquaint the candidate with its challenges, and to start the person on the path to finding a fulfilling and fulfilled life in the absence of sexual activity. The

---

each other's brothers and sisters. We are responsible for the consequences for our brethren of how we present ourselves, especially in an area as sensitive as that of sexual orientation. So, every brother should be accepted as he is. But the emergence of any sub-groups within a community, based on sexual orientation, would be highly divisive. It can threaten the unity of the community, it can make it harder for the brethren to practise the chastity which we have vowed. It can put pressure on brethren to think of themselves in a way that is not central to their vocation as preachers of the Kingdom, and which perhaps they may eventually discover to be untrue." Timothy Radcliffe, OP, *Sing a New Song: The Christian Vocation* (Dublin: Dominican Publications, 2000) 146–47.

whole of monastic life will be, for those who enter, a journey into chastity that will involve struggle and the expenditure of much energy in resisting temptation and in recovering confidence after failure. Monastic life is a way to becoming chaste; it does not necessarily demand that those who begin it are already perfect. It is part of the vocation director's duty to assess whether celibate chastity in the context of monastic life is a viable option for the candidate; this is not always a question with a simple binary answer. "It is important not to abdicate responsibility for psychosexual assessment to outside psychological consultants. Most psychologists consider *celibacy* to be abnormal!"[8]

7. Mostly, monastic life demands a reasonable degree of *physical health*, as is recognized by canon law (can. 642, CIC). To the extent that a community lifestyle calls for regular observance, daily work, and a fair degree of generosity, it is not usually a wise option for the fainthearted or the delicate. Sometimes even those who are robust find that their bodies rebel, letting them know they are in the wrong place. A thorough examination by a physician is a necessary prelude to entering. I have found it useful to ask that a fairly comprehensive form be filled out; otherwise, the physical examination can be rather superficial. There is a diversity of practice regarding screening for HIV and Hepatitis B and C.[9] It is important that each group have a policy on this that includes not only a decision on whether some or all candidates are to be tested but also what counseling is available, what response the community makes

---

8. Raymond F. Carey, "Pedophilia and Ephebophilia: Vocational Assessment Helps for Identifying 'At-Risk' Candidates," *VocNet* 5.3 (2002) 4.

9. On 23 July 1999, a comprehensive report on practice in Australia was circulated by (now-Bishop) Anthony Fisher, OP: "Report on HIV and Hepatitis Testing of Candidates for Priesthood and Religious Life."

to a positive result, and how the privacy of the procedures is protected.[10]

8. Linked with bodily health is *psychological health*, for the assessment of which we rely on a consultant psychologist.[11] It may well be that common sense and experience can arrive at a reasonable assessment of suitability, but something more can sometimes be helpful. This is because we often meet candidates when they are in good form and all is well with them. They do their best to project a positive image of themselves. We may have no experience of them when they are in a bad mood, disappointed, or resentful. Even if they try to present themselves as fully as they can, there are often areas of denial or repression in their lives that escape their own conscious scrutiny. We need psychologists to check beneath the surface. Often a certain amount of skill is required to read the resultant reports. Many psychologists use specialized software to analyze responses to psychometric tests and to generate a profile.[12] To avoid potential legal liability, the consultant will often include such tentative expressions as "this person may have such and such a tendency." Taken cumulatively, such statements often seem to present the candidate in a negative

---

10. James Keenan, "HIV Testing of Seminary and Religious-Order Candidates," *Review for Religious* 55.3 (1996) 297–314.

11. See Kevin E. McNamara, "Psychological Screening for Religious Life," *Review for Religious* 54.4 (1995) 589–93.

12. Difficulties can arise when, for various reasons, the candidate corresponds less closely to the control group from which the automated conclusions are drawn. Candidates for monastic life are rarely typical for their generation, especially if they have been living a quasi-monastic life on their own for some time. Some consider that a certain amount of caution is necessary when reliance is placed on projective tests such as the Rorschach. See Frederick Crews, "Out, Damned Blot!" *The New York Review of Books* 51.12 (15 July 2004) 22–25. This is a review of *What's Wrong with the Rorschach? Science Confronts the Controversial Inkblot Test*, by James M. Wood, M. Teresa Nezworski, Scott O. Lilienfeld, and Howard N. Garth. See also the correspondence in the edition of 4 November 2004, 64–65

light. Nobody escapes unscathed. It must be remembered that these conclusions are statistical probabilities, which may not take into account the special situation of one considering entrance into a monastery. Usually the recent history of life choices needs to be added to the mix as reliable indications of character over a period. This gives a dynamic picture that is often more revealing than a static snapshot. It is good to choose a consultant who is willing to enter into nondefensive discussion about the report in order to determine the relative seriousness of any problems. Some of the areas of concern may be the following:

> i. Often *depression* will be mentioned as a past event, a tendency, or a possibility. This is said to afflict up to 20 percent of the population at some time in their lives. As a result, some of those who present themselves for entry into monastic life may have been diagnosed as depressed and prescribed antidepressants. This may not always be significant, especially if the episode was mainly situational and if the diagnosis was made by a family physician rather than by a psychiatrist.[13] At the same time, during the history taking we should be aware of some of the common signs of depressive incidents.[14] Generally, bipolar disorder is more serious than simple depression and almost always recurrent; this is not always initially diagnosed. In milder cases, the extent of recovery and how a candidate may have handled the depression are not insignificant as pointers to character.

---

13. Note that overprescription of antidepressives is common. See Gail Bell, "The Worried Well: The Depression Epidemic and the Medicalisation of Our Sorrows," *Quarterly Essay* 18 (2005) 1–74.

14. Familiarity with the areas covered by such instruments as the *Beck Depression Inventory* or the *Kessler Psychological Distress Scale* can alert us to the possibility that a problem exists on which the consultant may be asked to comment. These instruments are easily available on the Internet.

ii. With *obesity* being widespread, some consideration may be needed to determine the extent to which this is regarded as merely a physical problem or as an indicator of underlying psychological problems. The same holds when anorexia is suspected.

iii. All *addictions* are to be taken seriously, whether they concern substance abuse, gambling, sex, or anything else. Whether the Internet or computer games are, strictly speaking, "addictive" is a disputed matter. Some of these activities manifest themselves as compulsive only when the opportunity to indulge them is removed.[15]

iv. With regard to *alcoholism*, no easy solution is available, but some knowledge of the disease and its indications is essential. It has been suggested that we should insist on up to ten years of sobriety before accepting an alcoholic candidate. Furthermore, in the case of acceptance we may need to make provision for ongoing contacts with AA.[16] More generally, formators may need to remain alert if they notice persons whose conversation includes such expressions as "I need a drink," and who regard alcohol as an appropriate response to stress.

v. In the case of serious *drug abuse*, professional advice should be sought, even if the person claims to have been cured.

vi. *Anger* sometimes settles not far beneath a placid surface, especially in those for whom social acceptance, in the past, implied compliance. Long-term anger is not always visible. Sometimes powerful but latent resentment is uncovered by projective tests. Therapy may be needed, but sometimes it is easier to persuade persons of this only after

---

15. See Gerald G. May, *Addiction and Grace: Love and Spirituality in the Healing of Addictions* (San Francisco: HarperSanFrancisco, 1991).

16. On the effect of alcoholism on community life, see Simon Peter, SJ, "Alcoholism and Jesuit Life: An Individual and Community Illness," *Studies in the Spirituality of Jesuits* 13.1 (January 1981) 1–66.

they themselves have become aware of the existence of anger within, whether by some growth in self-awareness or by an unexpected volcanic outburst.

vii. Any instance of *violence* or bullying behavior that may be expressive of a deep-seated tendency may warrant further investigation. Unknown to formators, bullying can occur in novitiates, at least in the form of chronic bossiness. For some, such behavior seems to be a compensation for the relative powerlessness in which they find themselves.[17]

viii. Excessive *abasement needs* can incline persons to enshrine themselves as resident victims and, later on, to claim exemptions and entitlements because of this. At first they seem unusually humble, docile, and obedient, at least externally. Later they become more demanding and, if their demands are not satisfied, resentful and prone to tantrums.

ix. *Sexual concerns* should always be conveyed to the consultant for further investigation. These days, it pays to be aware of the profile of a typical pedophile; the earlier potential pedophiles are detected and redirected, the better.

x. More recently the incidence of Asperger's syndrome has been noted among those interested in monastic life.[18]

---

17. See Gerald A. Arbuckle, *Dealing with Bullies: A Gospel Response to the Social Disease of Adult Bullying* (Strathfield: St Pauls, 2003).

18. "Many pine for the lifestyles that were adopted by monks in monasteries, where a calm tranquility allowed for routines in domestic life combined with solitary work." Simon Baron-Cohen, *Autism and Asperger Syndrome* (Oxford University Press, 2008) 48. The whole book is a good and simple explanation of the condition. See also, from the same author, *The Essential Difference: The Truth about the Male and Female Brain* (New York: Basic Books, 2003), esp. 133–54. See also Daniel Goleman, *Social Intelligence: The New Science of Human Relationships* (London: Hutchinson, 2006) 133–43. Recently, there is a degree of reluctance to classify Asperger Syndrome as a disorder; it is seen, rather, as a misunderstood particularity of brain operation that conflicts with current social expectations. "If Asperger's people are good systemisers and bad empathisers with extreme-male

Since depression is found in at least 50 percent of people with this condition,[19] sometimes their state is misdiagnosed as simple depression. Typically male, those who suffer the combination of social communication difficulties and a narrow band of interests, sometimes pursued relentlessly, plus a tendency toward repetitive actions, are now located on the autism spectrum. Their single-mindedness and total lack of empathy, their inability to appreciate humor or irony, their reluctance to do more than one thing at once, and their habitual anxiety and proneness to depression all usually demand much understanding from other members of the community. The condition is caused by neurobiological factors, and there is not much certainty about either its precise origin or the best treatment. In some cases, however, a bout of cognitive behavioral therapy has produced good results, and, in others, simple coaching can help.

9. Monastic communities without a specific apostolate have always been more flexible in the level of *education* required of those entering and have catered for a simple vocation as a lay brother or lay sister. Whether this is a viable option in the contemporary world is a question worth discussing. People interrupt their education for different reasons; an explanation

---

brains, the thought arises that there are probably people who are good empathisers and poor systemisers with extreme-female brains. A moment's thought will confirm that we all know such people, but their particular skill combination is rarely classified as pathological. It is probably easier to live a normal life in the modern world with poor systemising skills than with poor empathising skills. In the Stone Age, it might have been less easy." Matt Ridley, *Nature via Nurture: Genes, Experience and What Makes Us Human* (London: Fourth Estate, 2003) 62. On the many aspects of daily living touched by Asperger's syndrome and on ways of working toward creative outcomes, see Geoffrey Nutting, *On Becoming More Open to Others in God: Asperger Syndrome and the Enneagram* (DMin thesis, Melbourne College of Divinity, 2009).

19. Baron-Cohen, *Autism and Asperger Syndrome*, 98.

should be sought in the case of those whose education is incomplete. Those who have not been educated to their capacity before entry may, on the one hand, find some fulfillment in the opportunities offered in monastic life or, on the other, adopt an obscurantist attitude to further education that leaves them bitter and resentful for life.

10. Many communities have experience of those who have an extremely varied history of *employment*. This too seems to be a contemporary pattern. Generations X and Y are likely to change careers and employment several times in their lives,[20] and so it is not too surprising that after a successful university education and several years in one or two high-paying jobs, a person may conceive the ambition to enter monastic life. Beyond the search for higher rewards obvious among many, these changes of employment can also be driven by a sense of disenchantment with the lack of meaning offered and the search for positions that are characterized by greater vision, value, and purpose.

11. Some communities ask for a *police certificate* before entry. With older candidates who have lived a mobile life and for whom no lifetime referees are available, this may be prudent if it can be done without causing offense.

12. Saint Benedict's criterion of truly seeking God remains a powerful one. This has to have a solid foundation long before entry becomes a possibility. The regularity of *religious practice* must be insisted on, and every encouragement needs to be given to candidates to increase the fervor of their sacramental lives, attendance at Mass, parish involvement, and personal

---

20. It is thought that Generation X (1963–80) will average three careers and eight jobs in their working lives, Generation Y (1980–2000) five careers and 15 jobs. Mark Abernathy, *The Bulletin*, 1 November 2005.

prayer and reading. In the final analysis, it is a deep attraction to prayer and a capacity for solitary communion with God that will be the great generators of a good monastic life and ultimate perseverance.

13. Formerly, a sound *family background* was considered one of the primary conditions for acceptance into religious life. This sometimes had the effect of equating respectability with good nurturance; unconventional upbringings were not considered acceptable. Changes in society have led to many dysfunctional families—some mildly so, others severely. Divorce and parental remarriage are becoming more common, and this rupture often has a disturbing effect on the next generation. Here, as elsewhere, it is important to treat each person as an individual; some have acquired life-enhancing skills as the result of painfully negotiating family breakup, and the value of these should not be minimized. Inevitably, we will all carry the effects of primary socialization throughout life, and just as inevitably, these will be almost invisible to us, though often they will be patent to others. Our family has made us what we are, and we have to accept it and get on with life.

* * *

This formidable list of areas to be explored may seem to form an insurmountable barrier to entry into monastic life. Nobody is surprised that all who come to us will carry with them a certain number of liabilities. Mostly these are vocationally irrelevant, but it is useful to know about them since many of them will be met again and again in the formation process.

At some stage in the assessment or discernment process, I often make use of an instrument I have developed called "The Journey to Monastic Life." This involves asking the candidate to consider eight journeys that sometimes need to be made if a person is to make the transition from secular life to monastic life. Not everyone has to make every journey. Usually one or two stand out as in need of special attention in the period before formal admission takes place. The instrument is autodiagnostic: candidates are encouraged to work out which areas in their lives can be upgraded with a view to entering the monastery. They may wish to discuss their conclusions, but I do not insist on this. I do make the point that the journey or journeys they begin will continue all through life; they do not have to arrive at the end of the road before considering entry. This is another way of making them aware of some of the challenges involved in following the monastic path and in finding out for themselves whether they have the grit to pursue it. The possibilities are

1. the journey to self-knowledge,
2. the journey to self-disclosure,
3. the journey to community,
4. the journey to discipline of life,
5. the journey to celibacy,
6. the journey to the sacraments,
7. the journey to devotion, and
8. the journey to understanding.

The challenge facing vocation directors is to assist candidates in making the transition from suitability to readiness. Once objective suitability has been verified, we need to help them come to the conclusion that they have the will and the resources to make the transition.

It is possible for an assessment process to become bogged down in tracking and measuring negative qualities in the candidate. Even when an abundance of these is in evidence, they have to be viewed in the context of complementary positive qualities. The most obvious of these is the fact that the candidate has experienced an interior call to a particular way of life and, often, to a particular community. Add to this the pointer mentioned by Pope Paul VI in his message for Vocation Sunday in 1970: the inquirer is willing to take matters further and to take practical steps in pursuing religious life instead of forever hovering on the threshold.

The candidate for monastic life most likely to persevere will manifest a good working relationship among certain contrary qualities.

1. *Stability and Adaptability.* Stability in this case means a willingness to stay with the process after the initial shine has gone out of it, to accept that hard times are not necessarily an indication of having no vocation, and to be patient and prepared to take counsel until some clarity is attained. Adaptability means being prepared to change one's ways to correspond approximately to the expectations of community life and not to be rigid about ideals and practices that may have served well during pre-entry but will almost certainly need at least fine-tuning in the new situation. The image that best illustrates the dialectic between the qualities is the surfer on a surfboard. To continue standing is a matter not of inertness or rigidity but of continual adaptation to movement and readiness for the unexpected.

2. *Regularity and Creativity.* Monastic life works its magic by the medium of regularity; it is a disciplined life that yields results only with the passage of time. The purpose of the externally regular life, however, is to enable persons to concentrate more fully on the quality of what they do. Gustave Flaubert, the author of *Madame Bovary*, once wrote in a letter, "Be regular and ordinary in your life, like a bourgeois, so that you may be violent and original in your work." It is the interaction of opposite qualities that produces a good result. In a similar vein, Herbert von Karajan, the conductor of the Berlin Philharmonic Orchestra, admitted to being a superelitist because the only people he would admit into his orchestra were those who had the music in their souls *and* who played in time with others. I have often thought that this summarizes well the qualities we hope to find in candidates.

3. *Community and Solitude*. Monastic life is certainly an expression of the desire "to be alone with the Alone," and it requires the capacity for a good amount of silence, solitude, and sequestration. This does not mean that it is designed only for strong introverts. The genius of cenobitic life is that it sustains and supports the solitary search for God through the means of an affective community that allows the person's intimacy and generative needs to find expression. In practice it often seems that introverts are trained to become more extroverted and extroverts helped to become more introverted; in each case a more complete human being is the aim.

4. *Self-Knowledge and Compassion*. Self-knowledge is of prime importance in monastic life, and it comes about from years of experience, from living in community, and from wise counsel. The self-knowledge that is the effect of a burgeoning spiritual life is not so much the fruit of sustained introspection as of the serene and confident recognition of the humanity shared with others. "I am a human being, and nothing that is human is foreign to me."[21] Far from being narcissistic self-concern, genuine self-knowledge progressively opens up the way to understanding, empathy, and compassion and reaches its paradoxical peak in self-forgetfulness.

In the final analysis, the pragmatic question to be asked is whether the formator and the candidate realistically judge that they can work together creatively. Neither is without character flaws or weaknesses; the question is, "Are these of such magnitude that they would impede the process of monastic formation?" The capacity of different formators to cope with such potential impediments varies; some have a higher tolerance than others. There does not need to be perfect temperamental compatibility or immediate intimacy between formator and candidate, but just the sense that both are of

---

21. Terence, *Heauton timoroumenos*, 25.

sufficient maturity to collaborate actively in their respective tasks. In any case, we often learn more from those who maintain a professional distance than from those in whose presence we are completely comfortable.

Abbot André Louf, a perceptive and experienced spiritual guide, makes the point that a person's negative qualities may have a positive contribution to make on the unfolding of a vocation:

> No one has to be a novice master or a psychologist to admit without difficulty that the ideal candidate for religious life, someone who presents only positive qualities, does not exist—fortunately! But we can say more: in the discernment of a vocation, what is important is not the positive qualities of a personality but its negative aspects, or rather the way in which these negative aspects are lived out relative to a vocation. This is because—and this is extremely important—if there is a vocation from God, this vocation will lean just as much on the negative aspects of the candidate's psychology as on the positive.[22]

This sentiment is echoed by Pope Benedict XVI in his 2006 message for Vocation Sunday: "To respond to God's call and set out, it is not necessary to be already perfect. . . . Human limitations and fragility are not an obstacle, on the condition that they make us ever more aware that we need God's redeeming love."[23] This principle is worth pondering.

Accepting the Unacceptable

Having set up barriers to exclude those who are unsuitable, perhaps we should begin to consider making exceptions to the rules that we have so comprehensively formulated. God does

---

22. André Louf, *Grace Can Do More: Spiritual Accompaniment and Spiritual Growth* (Kalamazoo, MI: Cistercian Publications, 2002) 64.

23. *Osservatore Romano* (weekly edition in English), 12 April 2006, 5.

not always follow our guidelines; whatever our experiences or preferences, the primary requirement of good vocation directors is that they try to discern God's will rather than impose their own.

Sometimes, in working with monastic formators, I have offered a couple of provocative case studies. In most discussions the candidates proposed have been considered unsuitable. It is at this point that I reveal their names: Saint Bernard of Clairvaux and Thomas Merton. I am not suggesting that either of these giants would have been easy people to deal with; I am merely making the point that monasticism would have been impoverished if they had been rejected. This is not because I am unrealistic or naïve, but it does seem true that if we make mediocrity the norm in our acceptance of candidates, we are likely to end up with mediocre communities. My belief is that we should not be too quick to exclude those who do not correspond to our mental picture of what a prospective candidate should be like; this would be to underestimate the transformative power of monastic life.

Here are two case studies. The first is a story told about a candidate acquired by Saint Bernard of Clairvaux:

> It happened once that the same servant of God had to approach Count Theobald on some business. When he approached the town where he then was, he met a large crowd of people who, on the Count's order, were dragging a wicked and notorious bandit to his punishment. When the most kind Father saw this, he grasped with his hand the thongs by which he was bound and said to his executioners, "Release this murderer to me, for I want to hang him with my own hands." When the Count heard of the arrival of the man of God, he hurried there to meet him, for he had always loved and honored him devotedly. When he saw the rope in his hand by which he was dragging the bandit behind him, he was horrified and said, "Alas, reverend Father, what are you wanting to do? Why are you trying to call back this rogue, a thousand times convicted, back from the gate of

hell? Can you save one who has totally become a devil? His amendment is hopeless. The only good that can be done is his death. Allow, therefore, this lost man to go to his doom since while he is alive the lives of many are in danger."

The venerable Father replied and said, "I know this, O best of men, I know that this man is a most heinous bandit and that he deserves the fiercest torments. Do not think that I wish to allow this kind of sinner to go unpunished. I am thinking of handing him over to torturers to receive his due retribution in an appropriate manner, but one that lasts longer. You have sentenced him to a quick punishment to be completed by an instantaneous death, but I will make him die by a long-lasting crucifixion and a slow death. You let him hang for one day on the gallows and remain hanging on the gibbet for many days. I will nail him to a cross for several years to live in perpetual punishment and then to die."

When this most Christian prince heard this, he was silent and he did not dare to argue further against the words of the saint. Immediately, therefore, this kindest Father took off his tunic and clothed the prisoner with it and, having cut his hair, joined him in companionship with the Lord's sheepfold, making a lamb out of a sheep, a lay brother out of a bandit. Coming with him to Clairvaux, he was obedient until death, surviving, if I am not mistaken, thirty or more years in the Order. He was called Constantius, a man whom we ourselves have seen and known.[24]

That such events were possible only in the Middle Ages is contradicted by a more recent story, that of Br. Gregory Bernier of the Cistercian abbey of Sainte-Marie du Désert. Born in 1917, he was in and out of prison until, in 1944, he was sent to a labor camp in Germany. At war's end, he resumed his criminal activities: burglary, assault with a deadly weapon, and other offenses. Between 1938 and 1957 he spent a dozen years in a variety of prisons. Eventually he ended up in jail on the island of Ré, off the coast of La Rochelle, in a former

---

24. Herbert of Clairvaux, *De miraculis*, 2:15; PL 185, 1324–25.

Cistercian monastery transformed into a prison for hard cases. Here he underwent a conversion. Released in 1957, he went directly to the monastery of Désert and, after a few weeks in the guest house, was admitted into the novitiate as a lay brother, eventually to be solemnly professed in 1963. He died on 22 August 2002; he was eighty-five years old, forty-five of which were spent in the monastery. In many ways he was a model monk and, it seems, a fulfilled human being.[25]

Character is what matters—the history of choices. This history needs to be assessed not as a static reality but as something constantly moving and changing. What we hope to determine is the direction and intensity of the choices being made at the present. Sometimes a substantial conversion gives a greater dynamism to a vocational choice than a tepid realignment of trivialities. Character is more important than past liabilities or minor neuroses, which tend to multiply the deeper the investigation goes. A community already tolerates some odd characters; a few more will not make much difference! Indeed, giving priority to the acceptance of weak and wounded people is an important way of not only ensuring that the community receives new members but also enhancing the affective quality of the common life.

In this Aelred of Rievaulx offers us a good example:

> [Aelred] turned the house of Rievaulx into a stronghold for the sustaining of the weak and the nurturing of the strong and perfect, for the atmosphere of peace and fraternal love [*pietas*], and for the cultivation of the fullest charity toward God and the neighbor. Who did not find there a place of quiet, be he most abject and worthy of contempt? Who ever came there weak and did not find paternal love in Aelred, and in the brothers the consolation he needed? Who was ever expelled from that house because he was frail of body

---

25. See Robert Masson, *C'était un larron: du banditisme à La Trappe* (Paris: Parole et Silence, 2009).

or character—unless his iniquity was a source of offense to the whole community or a threat to his own salvation? So it was that monks who needed fraternal mercy and compassion flocked to Rievaulx from foreign nations and from the farthest ends of the earth came to Rievaulx, and finding the doors open, they freely entered there giving praise to the Lord.[26]

The same priorities are visible in an Advent discourse given by Aelred when he was Abbot of Revesby. The community was made up not of pious clones but of people of varied backgrounds, some of them unsavory:

> Consider how God has gathered you together in this place, from vastly different regions and from different lifestyles. One of you, when he was in the world, was like a lion, who despised others and thought himself better than them because of his pride and riches. Another was like a wolf, who lived from robbery and whose only interest was how to steal the property of others. A leopard is an animal marked by variety: such were some of you [who lived] by your wits, through deception and fraud. Furthermore, there were many in this community who were foul because of their sexual sins. Such as these were like goats—because goats are foul animals. There were some of you who lived innocent lives when you were in the world; they may well be compared to lambs. There were others who were like sheep because you lived a simple life. Look now, brothers, and see with how much concord and peace God has gathered all these into one common life. Here the wolf lives with the lamb; he eats and drinks with the lamb and does him no harm but loves him greatly. There is no doubt that he who was a wolf when he was in the world now lives with great concord with the one who was as innocent as a lamb.

---

26. Walter Daniel, *The Life of Aelred of Rievaulx*, ed. Maurice Powicke (Oxford: Clarendon Press, 1978) XXIX, 36–37. See also Christophe Michaud, "The Power of Strength and the Power of Weakness," *Tjurunga* 58 (2000) 71–88.

He who was proud as a lion now lives in great peace and quiet with one who through simplicity was and is a sheep. Here it happens that not only does the lion remain with the calf, but what is more marvelous, the lion becomes a calf.[27]

There is always the possibility that those whom we assess as unsuitable monastic candidates may yet be discerned as having a genuine call from God to enter a monastery. But caution is recommended; we cannot afford to be naïve.

---

27. Aelred of Rievaulx, *Sermon* 1:33–35; CCCM 2A, 10–11.

Chapter Seven

BUILDING TRUST

The only environment in which effective monastic formation can occur is that of mutual trust and fidelity. A candidate who trusts the tradition, the community, the superior, and the formators will have much less difficulty in being open and receptive to what they have to offer. There is a difficulty. Especially in contemporary circumstances, unlimited trust cannot be assumed. It has to be built. In this chapter I would like to ponder different strategies that may contribute to the realization of this objective.[1]

Out of fairness to those expressing an interest in joining monastic life, it is important that the various stages of the relationship be in substantial harmony. Those with the responsibility for formation will need to ensure that, from the very first contact, there is no confusion about the nature of monastic life or about the specific identity of a particular community, including its limits and demands. This will often mean ensuring that promotional literature is not too lyrical and does not promise more than the monastery can deliver. Saint Benedict's suggestion is probably the best: no attempt should be made to paint monastic life in rosy hues; instead, its challenges should be clearly set forth. "Let all the hard and rough

---

1. In this chapter, trust is being approached from the direction of the formator or superior. It could also be approached from the other direction. There is no doubt that many newcomers have serious psychological difficulties with trust: they have never learned to have confidence in others, or they have learned not to have confidence in them, or, less usually, they may give their trust cheaply so that there is no real depth to it. For those who have suffered the trauma of some kind of abuse, building trust requires much effort and a good deal of patience.

things by which the journey to God is made be told him in advance" (RB 58.8). This is especially important in the case of those who are attracted by the æsthetics of monastic life; the reality may come as something of a shock.

Whether a policy is written once and for all or continually updated, there needs to be a clear understanding between those responsible for formation and the community, as well as among the formators themselves. This coherence is especially the task of the superior, who, although not immediately involved in the daily details of formation, has an important role in monitoring the progress of new members and in making sure that they are growing into the community practically, affectively, and intellectually. The superior's teaching to the whole community, the policies implemented in the house, and sustained personal interaction are essential components of formation. The superior also needs to be willing to support formators in their sometimes demanding task and to be a peacemaker when conflicts arise either among formators or between formators and those in their charge.[2]

---

2. Speaking of the importance of an additional or backup person in the formative relationship, André Louf writes, "The classic case comes in the sometimes excellent and sometimes difficult, but always delicate, collaboration between the novice master and the major superior, abbot or provincial. This collaboration is all the more delicate in the Benedictine family, where the novice master exercises his office—at least in theory—subordinate to the Father Abbot, to whom Tradition confides a kind of global spiritual fatherhood over the whole life of the monastery, novices included. This vision of things no doubt conforms to Tradition and deserves respect. Psychologically, however, it is important that the novice master's role be fully promoted so that there can be no doubt in the novice's eyes about the dominant role he exercises. Having two Fathers is not good, or even thinkable, for the novice. The abbot's role is not obscured or avoided for all that. In addition to his deep communion with the novice master, which must be obvious to everyone, by his simple presence the abbot will contribute positively to the novice's spiritual growth, without any need to say a lot of things or hold periodic interviews which might easily be a source of

With several persons responsible for different aspects or stages of formation, there is a need for the harmonious operation of a group that meets regularly. Such a gathering can operate as a support group for the formators, but it also makes possible a good level of continuity between the various stages of formation. Tactics for dealing with persons perceived as difficult can be discussed and evaluated. Inevitably there will be different styles and different gifts among formators; this can be of benefit to those in their care. If one is perceived as less sympathetic, another may be able to remedy that deficiency. In the monastic tradition of the Eastern Church, newcomers receive two personal formators, one designated to act as a father, challenging and correcting, the other as a mother, encouraging and affirming. It is a good reminder that despite our efforts to be "all things to all people" we may not, on our own, be able to provide all that is needed. The key to the effectiveness of such a group is cooperation and complementarity, with no room left for competition or subversion. It is for the superior to give positive leadership in this matter.

Often formators have cause to discuss among themselves the openness of particular persons. Sometimes this refers to the capacity for self-revelation, an ease in talking about intimate aspects of personal history or present temptations. At other times it means the person's willingness to embrace the life of the community in its integrity. In both meanings those beginning monastic life will make no progress unless they are able to trust the community and those who serve as formators.

The trust given by those newly come to monastic life is a very fragile quality. Formed under the influence of postmodernism, there is a widespread and preemptive suspiciousness concerning authority. Whatever is done officially is presumed to have potentially adverse effects for those outside the power structures. Even with regard to casual relationships, trust can-

---

confusion to the novice." *Grace Can Do More: Spiritual Accompaniment and Spiritual Growth* (Kalamazoo, MI: Cistercian Publications, 2002) 154.

not be taken for granted—it needs to be earned. This is what Robert D. Putnam writes in *Bowling Alone*:

> Our youth are, in effect, telling us that in their experience most people *aren't* trustworthy. Perhaps thick trust—confidence in personal friends—is as strong as ever, as some Gen. X'ers believe. However, thin trust—the tenuous bond between you and your nodding acquaintance from the coffee shop, that crucial emollient for large, complex societies like ours—is becoming rarer.[3]

Benjamin Chaminade is a business consultant who has concentrated on the difficulty many businesses have in retaining their valued employees—a problem not unknown also in religious life. His solution is simple to enunciate: it is necessary to build up a climate of mutual trust, expressed in good levels of communication and, more specifically, in genuine listening on the part of management. The term he uses for this is *fidélisation:*

> *Fidélisation* is the voluntary action by which a business establishes an environment that maintains the attachment of the employee over a long period. This enduring and constant attachment that binds the employee to the business is based on shared values. Putting in place a policy of *fidélisation* consists in placing persons and their expectations at the heart of the business concerns so that the professional satisfaction of the employee is assured and a relationship of mutual confidence is established.[4]

The lesson for monastic communities is that we have to be active in earning and securing the trust of those who enter. This is done especially through good communication, sustained listening, and fair dealing.

---

3. Robert D. Putnam, *Bowling Alone: The Collapse and Revival of American Community* (New York: Simon & Schuster, 2001) 142.

4. Benjamin Chaminade, "Fidélisation versus retention," 8 June 2003, translated from www.focusrh.com/article.php3?id_article=107.

In his wide-ranging book *The Speed of Trust* Stephen M. R. Covey speaks of trust in terms of a bank account. Some actions will increase the amount of trust; others will decrease it. The bad news is that actions that reduce trust have a greater impact than those that build it up. Generally, trust is built up by competence in the area of responsibility. What destroys trust is not incompetence so much as perceived defects of character.[5] These may or may not be real; the effect is the same. Rebuilding trust after a breakdown is an onerous task; it will often involve reinventing oneself, at least in the eyes of another.

The primary component of a good formation situation is a high level of trust. The crucial questions are these: How may this trust be built? How may it be rebuilt? Reflection on our own experience will be instructive—what it felt like when someone trusted us, and what kind of experiences caused us to become mistrustful. At the risk of overwhelming the reader, here are eight ways of acting that can create an environment in which newcomers will be likely to relax and absorb what is offered to them.

1. *Giving Honor.* Honor is an important quality in a Benedictine community. All people are to be honored (RB 4.8), especially those seemingly unworthy of it (RB 53.7; 53:15). In particular, the monks are to anticipate one another in giving honor (RB 72.4). Honor is more than courtesy or respect, important though these attitudes are. To be honored by others, especially by superiors, is an important component in job satisfaction, in building healthy self-esteem, and in keeping morale at a high level.[6] To live in disgrace is to be rejected; it blocks

---

5. Stephen M. R. Covey, with Rebecca R. Merrill, *The Speed of Trust: The One Thing That Changes Everything* (New York: Free Press, 2006) 130–33. See also his father, Stephen R. Covey, "The Voice of Trustworthiness—Modeling Character and Competence," in *The 8th Habit: From Effectiveness to Greatness* (New York: Free Press, 2005) 146–85.

6. See the interview with Fr. Stephen Rossetti, author of *The Joy of Priesthood* (Notre Dame: Ave Maria Press, 2005), where he correlates support and affirmation

the expression of the social element in human nature and is, therefore, an impediment to human happiness and fulfillment. This is why, in some cultures, death is preferred to dishonor.

Honor exceeds respect as much as respect exceeds politeness. Politeness is a matter of extending to others the courtesies common in a particular civilization; in its more sophisticated forms it may develop into urbanity, as distinct from rusticity. Politeness is a form of self-containment that shapes our behavior so that we deal with others in accordance with the best social conventions of our culture. Respect is more interior. It is an attitude rather than a behavior. It is a recognition and an esteem of the special qualities that others possess: their sporting prowess, their ease with technology, their driving skills. Our behavior toward this other person is driven by this attitude. I may not like a particular person very much, but I may respect her skill in writing sonnets. So, when I am in dire need of a sonnet, it is to her that I make my request rather than asking others for whom my feelings may be warmer.

Honor is something even deeper. It is a quality that is inseparable from humility. When I honor others, it is as though I abase myself before them. According to Saint Benedict, the honor to be given to guests is to be shown by humility, by bowing the head or prostrating the whole body on the ground. Such a radical attitude is not merely ceremonial; it follows the perception that, in some mysterious manner, Christ is present in the stranger (RB 53.6-8). It is not looking through the stranger to see Christ, as though the stranger is not important and the honor is given to Christ alone. It is, rather, recognizing that as much honor as is due to Christ is due to the unprepossessing wanderer who has arrived on our doorstep.

Speaking of the attitude of superiors to those in their care, the Second Vatican Council stated, "They should govern those under them as sons [or daughters] of God, respecting them

---

received by priests from their bishops with job satisfaction and high morale. *Our Sunday Visitor*, 9 October 2005, 5.

as human beings."[7] This means recognizing their dignity as adult persons, not treating them as children or as persons to be tamed by bureaucratic measures or constrained by physical or emotional force. For those who take this declaration at its face value, holding office in religious life can no longer be seen as permission for authoritarian bossiness. It is, rather, an invitation to treat people with more respect than we might have shown otherwise, and, to go further, it is to honor them for what they are. The Rule of Benedict guarantees to all, including newcomers, that they will be taken seriously, that their gifts will be recognized and used (RB 57), that their genuine needs will be met (RB 34.1-5; 37), that they will not be subject to arbitrary violence or bullying (RB 70), and that they have the right of appeal against burdensome or impossible commands (RB 69). There are constraints placed upon the exercise of authority as safeguards against the violation of the dignity of those who have voluntarily placed themselves "under a rule and an abbot."

The recognition of human dignity is important in Christian tradition and is, for example, a frequent theme in the sermons of Saint Leo the Great. Honoring others goes beyond even this. When I honor others, I appreciate their uniqueness, and so I reduce myself and my self-assertion in order to make room for them. I step back so that they have more space in which to expand. When the pope comes to visit, I honor him by giving him the best seat, allowing him to control the flow of the conversation while I sit quietly by giving him my full attention, like Mary of Bethany. If I do speak, it is gently and seriously in few and reasonable words. Before such greatness my lesser eminence fades into insignificance. He must increase and I must decrease.

This is how I am to honor other persons as well. I evacuate the common space and allow them to occupy it. I am fully

---

7. *Perfectæ Caritatis,* 14; Sacrosanctum Œcumenicum Concilium Vaticanum II, *Constitutiones, Decreta, Declarationes* (Vatican City: Libreria Editrice Vaticana, 1966) 346.

present, not mentally elsewhere. I do not monopolize the conversation with repetitive monologues. I do not fill the air with stentorian tones but speak quietly. I do not seek to impose my own will on the other but engage in what Saint Benedict terms "mutual obedience" (RB 71), giving priority to what the other person wishes (RB 72.4). I do not procrastinate over their requests or keep them waiting unnecessarily. If I can show honor to the pope, there is no reason why I cannot do it for everybody else.

I have had the privilege of meeting holy people. On each occasion I have been greatly edified by the graciousness with which they treat others, irrespective of their standing. The greater bows down before the lesser. This is done in all simplicity, without any semblance of subterfuge or hypocrisy. Such moments have reminded me of the Lord washing the feet of his disciples, not as empty ritual or as a pedagogical gesture but in an act full of love and honor. It is difficult to express what is experienced by the recipient of such honor—it is as though this holy person has pierced through the outward tegument and looked into the depths of the soul, finding there something great, beautiful, and worthy of honor. It is as though consent is being given to that inner person to exist and an invitation extended to come forth and flourish. In a world where we are surrounded by much misunderstanding and many hostile projections, someone has glimpsed who we really are and loved us.

Honor gives others the permission to exist; it encourages the emergence of what is hidden, and it provides a nurturing environment in which the inner self may become more visible and active. For newcomers, such a deeply welcoming community gives them the possibility of shedding the false identity that they may have carried many years, and so they gradually learn to become what they are: not just a stereotypical monk or nun produced by the monastic assembly line but a unique expression of the monastic charism, yet one that bears the imprint of the community that formed it.

One of those who recognized the importance of mutual honor in monastic life was the seventeenth-century reformer of the monastery of La Trappe, Abbot Armand-Jean de Rancé. He saw the giving of honor to others through mutual obedience as an excellent way of curbing the impulses of self-will and self-aggrandizement. But there was a theological underpinning to his thought. We honor the brother because God also has honored him. "You must consider your brothers," de Rancé wrote, "as people who carry on their foreheads the imprint of a blessing. They belong to Jesus Christ by a very special consecration. They are destined for his service in a unique way. They are precious vessels in his house."[8]

A community that genuinely honors those who enter has great power of influence. The honor that goes beyond courtesy or hospitality encourages newcomers to be themselves, to allow themselves to be seen as they are, and eventually to become themselves in the fullest possible sense.

2. *Giving Time.* The most practical way in which I honor others is by making myself available for them, giving them that most precious of commodities: my time. We can usually find time for important people, for those who have something to offer us, or for those who amuse us. It is important that we learn to expand the boundaries of this selective availability. This may well mean that our time is less governed by agenda and more open to the surprises that are ready to unfold in each moment. That we experience this as an impossible ideal indicates how much we are driven by real and imagined urgencies and how close we may often be to disregarding something that is really important.

Being available means being prepared to engage with others where they are, and that means moving out of our own space

---

8. Armand-Jean de Rancé, *La Régle de saint Benoist nouvellement traduite et éxpliquée selon son véritable esprit*, vol. 2 (Paris: François Muguet and George & Louis Josse, 1689) 557–58.

into theirs. It means putting our own needs and activities on hold while we offer hospitality to another. The way we do this is by being open to participate in conversation. This is not the idle chatter that the Rule of Saint Benedict so often rejects but a sensible adult exchange that gives expression to the truth of the relationship, massages away or preempts many misunderstandings, and lubricates future dealings lest unnecessary friction occur. The content may be trivial and unremembered, but the metamessage is one of welcome and respect. The more these agreeable conversations take place with mature members of the community, the more the subtle reshaping of the newcomer's values advances.

A recognition of the positive role of adult conversation is now more commonly welcomed among theologians, especially in England. Dialogue is proposed not only as a means of attaining a fuller human maturity but also as an essential means of evangelization in a pluralistic world:

> The Christian Church is best understood as a schooling in conversation. Such a schooling is necessary because truthful converse requires the recognition that the "self" who speaks must first be heard by others in order to be a self at all. It requires that I recognize others as themselves constitutive of my own identity. To be a self requires a mutuality of trust that permits the risk of recognizing my inescapable interdependence on others. In order to find myself, I must dispossess myself.[9]

We often underestimate the skill required to become adept in this art. We can learn a lot from the salon culture of seventeenth-century France.[10] A good conversationalist is not

---

9. Gerard Loughlin, reviewing Rowan Williams' *On Christian Theology*, in *Times Literary Supplement*, 4 August 2000.

10. See Peter France, "The Pleasure of Their Company," *The New York Review of Books* 52.11 (23 June 2005) 18; a review of Benedetta Craveri, *The Age of Conversation* (New York: New York Review Books, 2005).

what is called in Australia an "earbasher"—one who is always ready to talk insistently and for a long time, not registering the tedium on listeners' faces. Such a person inevitably dominates any group, doing aural violence to those constrained to listen. A good conversationalist is prepared to let others have their turn to speak. As is often said, we have two ears and only one tongue: we should listen twice as much as we speak. A skillful conversationalist seeks harmony in the group rather than confrontation and is not boring or hurtful but witty and inclusive. People walk away after a good conversation with a spring in their step, confirmed in their selfhood and in their solidarity with the group.

I do not know how advocating quality conversation in a monastery can be reconciled with the traditional monastic insistence on silence. I think this is a case where we must try to hold together opposite values. If mutuality is recognized as an essential component of effective and affective community, I do not see how mutuality can be achieved without a solid level of adult interaction. In general there is much more need for speech in monastic life today; monks and nuns expect to be kept informed of what is happening, they expect that regular channels of communication will exist between the leadership and the rest, and they believe that when situations of conflict arise they can often be resolved only by patient negotiation.

A newcomer becomes acquainted with a community through conversation, and it is by this means that the members of the community signal their acceptance. This is a situation that slowly builds trust and allows the newcomer to feel at home in the monastery, despite the distance between generations. The importance of the conversations between newcomers and their formators will be explored at length in a later chapter.

3. *Listening*. We are assailed from all sides by admonitions to practice the art of listening: Saint Benedict's Rule, Carl Rogers's nondirective approach to counseling, even studies

in management.[11] "Today's leader must be one who embraces listening as the principal guide for direction."[12] An attitude of listening is torture for some people, and for most it sometimes (at least) requires both discipline and concentration. Genuine listening goes beyond dozily uh-huhing through fifty minutes of unreflective babble. It is more active than passive. It seeks to get beneath the surface to uncover what the speaker means by the words used and what is being communicated through what is unsaid. Active listening contributes something. It is not simply silent before the spoken word of the other. Rather, it continually invites the spoken word to reshape itself in such a way that it brings fresh insight to the speaker.

We should not be too confident in our ability to apprehend immediately what the speaker wishes us to hear. Language often conceals as much as it reveals. Sometimes this is deliberate. Usually it is because many persons have poor skills in communicating what they are feeling and, even more so, what they are experiencing spiritually. If we do not hear what they are trying to say, the failure will be attributed by them to our poor listening, not to their inadequate powers of self-expression. And so trust is lost. To gain trust we need to work hard to grasp what the other person is trying to communicate, to check that we have really understood, and to respond in a manner that communicates a positive feeling of understanding and acceptance.

It can happen that we fail to hear what the other is saying because we do not want to hear it. We fear that picking up the message will oblige us to take action. We do not want to hear that others are unhappy, that they feel exploited, victimized, or abused, because this will project us into an unpleasant situation. So we allow the first subtle indications of dissatisfaction

---

11. See Stephen R. Covey, "Seek First to Understand, Then to be Understood," in *The Seven Habits of Highly Effective People* (Melbourne: The Business Library, 1990) 235–60.

12. Esther Fangman, osb, "Listening Turns the Soul to God," *Benedictines* 63.2 (2010) 13.

or discontent to sail over our heads, hoping that if we ignore them, they will go away. Maybe they will. Maybe these issues will never again be raised with us. This is hardly a cause for self-congratulation; we have missed an opportunity to enter into the area of another person's deep feelings. We have been offered an opportunity to gain the other person's trust, and we have let it pass us by.

I once heard a deceased abbot compared favorably with his living successor, and the speaker used the words, "You could say anything to him." It meant, I suppose, that there was a real freedom to express what one was feeling even though it may have been unpalatable and disturbing. There were no warning signs that flashed the message, "Go no further." Administrators who reflexively block any communication that may bring unwelcome news will quickly lose the trust of those under them, and the situation will become only worse. Body language is important here. Persons who are comfortable in their own skin, who have a solid self-knowledge, will not be uncomfortable with anything they hear from others. They will be grateful for the fuller truth, and they will be more aware of a sense of compassion for another's troubles than of their own helplessness to do anything to improve the situation.

One of the great obstacles to listening is the implicit belief (especially among men) that when a problem is presented, one has an obligation to solve it, to make things better, to find a remedy. It can seem as though for each difficulty mentioned there should be a pop-up solution. Sometimes people subtly communicate the message that they do not want to hear about anything they cannot deal with. Really bad situations make them feel useless and irrelevant. This is not a good attitude. We can make things better by simply listening and hearing. We cannot reverse history or undo a wrong. We cannot cure leprosy by a regal touch. No serious problem deserves an immediate response. First we have to listen and hear and feel. By providing rapid solutions, we take ourselves out of solidarity with the pain of others and establish ourselves as apart from them. A time may come for active solutions, but it is not now. First we have to listen.

Trust is built by listening, mistrust by failing to listen and by failing to hear what is said. By making time for others and extending the invitation to speak of what is closest to their hearts, we are building bridges that can sustain a high volume of traffic, if the occasion warrants it. In this way, both parties are growing in mutual trust and mutual commitment that will, in an undramatic way, be a channel by which the monastic charism is shared and nurtured, not only in them but also in us.

4. *Valuing Talents*. People inevitably feel unhappy when their specific talents are not recognized and appreciated. Valuing talents is, in Benjamin Chaminade's view, a key component of management and an essential element in retaining valued employees. A person will not become fully involved in common projects when much of what they have to give seems to be disregarded. There are relatively few key positions in a monastery, and most of those who hold them cling to them with great tenacity.[13] This is the glass-ceiling effect. There is no room

---

13. "As we all know, the kinds of service that allow one to feel like a 'leading actor' in some area are few in the monastery: the abbot or abbess, novice director, cellarer, cantor or chantress. This means that many monks and nuns of generative age find no place to channel their potential, which may lead to a sense of frustration affecting themselves and others. We might make a distinction here according to gender, even though not everyone will accept it. In nuns' monasteries, it would appear that the generative capacity is the exclusive domain of the Mother Abbess, or, by remote extension, of another sister in her immediate orbit. In monks' monasteries, other fathers (with a lower-case 'f') are allowed, even though there is only one Father Abbot. To put it more concretely, there is not always sufficient room or outlet for the generative capacity proper to adult professed monks and nuns, understood in general terms as the role of affirming and orienting the following generation. Not uncommonly, this is a source of crises and setback on the way to human and spiritual maturity. Even celibacy and

for parvenus, no matter how well qualified they may be. Even after several years, those coming to a community sometimes find it difficult to break into particular closed circles, whether they are social, administrative, or professional. The message given is that they do not really belong; they will probably have to wait for a vacancy to occur by death, departure, or promotion before some reluctant gesture of inclusion is offered.

To gain the trust of those who come to us, we have to create a culture that cherishes the gifts of each member of the community and encourages their employment for the benefit of all. Difficulties arise when the talents do not match the needs of the community. Someone who is fluent in Arabic, who has climbed Mt. Everest, or who has made hats for the queen of England will not find much occasion to exercise those specific aptitudes in most monasteries. Such people understand this when they decide to enter the monastery. What is needed is the sensible recognition of prior learning and an effort made to transfer the training into an activity that serves the common purpose. Thus, the Arabic speaker might end up teaching Hebrew, the mountain climber in charge of a fitness program, and the milliner transformed into a monastic tailor. Even if the skill itself is not directly usable, we can let these people know that we appreciate the character and dedication shown in acquiring it.

What is really at stake here is the warmth of the community reception and the completeness of the acceptance given to newcomers by members of the community and its leadership. When we respect their talents that they have worked at developing, we communicate our esteem for them. This goes

---

virginity for the sake of the Kingdom can end up being lived out in a castrating way. Frustrated generativity causes withdrawal into oneself, obsessive search for intimacy, invalidity at an early age, excessive worry about oneself. On the contrary, a positive living-out of generativity opens horizons, provides mutual enrichment, increases vital human energy, all of which brings with it an appetite for living." Bernardo Olivera, "Our Young and Not So Young Monks and Nuns," Conference given at the OCSO General Chapters, September 2002.

beyond the talents themselves; it says to them that we cherish them as persons.

It is not enough to value the talents of a few people, of our own inner circle. This tends to create a greater volume of resentment in those who are outside the circle and gives rise to a suspicion of favoritism. There needs to be an honest effort not only to recognize the talents that people believe they have but also to see potential for flourishing that is invisible to the persons themselves. An ongoing pastoral strategy that manifests a universal concern for providing opportunities for the development and employment of talents will have a good chance of earning widespread trust among members of the community.

Related to the recognition of talent is the expression of appreciation for the contributions made by individuals to the common good. There are many in monasteries who feel that their special gifts go unremarked and that their contribution to community life is undervalued, pending their funeral eulogy. It is probably true that it is all too easy to take people for granted and not to concern ourselves much with them unless they are visibly struggling or unless they complain. It is difficult to know how to remedy this, since a public statement can be experienced as hollow and even hypocritical when it is not the expression of a sincere sentiment. Even so, conventional expressions of gratitude and common courtesies are important ways of signaling our appreciation to others; we should be aware that their omission is noticed and felt.

5. *Speaking Truthfully*. Although we have noted that truth is a rubbery reality with many of those raised in the last half century, such people do demand a high level of credibility from those with positions of responsibility in the community. They have grown up with the presupposition that political figures habitually spin the truth until it has transformed itself into good news. They expect something better from those who wield religious authority.

Outright deceit and telling lies are not the only ways of failing to speak the truth. The trust of others is jeopardized when we withhold information or present it so steeped in interpretation that it is unrecognizable, when we rebaptize something to make it seem like something else, when we reconstruct the narrative to suit the audience. Honesty is ultimately the best policy. An unpleasant truth remains unpleasant however we describe it. By disguising the truth, we make our communication less offensive to others and save ourselves from having to face their anger, but when the facts are fully known, our credibility is damaged. Being plainspoken does not entail being rude or offensive; combined with respect, it can only enhance the relationship. Consider a physician who has to communicate a diagnosis of a life-threatening disease. It is a challenging task, but if it is done clearly and sensitively, it will probably increase the level of trust, even though the news is bad.

Even more corrosive of credibility is the habit of delivering different messages to different people, so that what is spoken of approvingly to one is disparaged to another. When members of a community compare notes, they are led to conclude that someone is not telling the whole truth. They may not be able to prove perjury in a court of law, but another seed of cynicism is sown, and the task of building up trust becomes harder. It is important that we speak about those who are absent as if they were present, not saying to a third party anything we would not say directly to them.[14]

Superiors and others who hold authority in monastic life sometimes have the difficult obligation to "speak the truth in love" (Eph 4:15). This involves pointing out unacceptable behavior either privately or publicly. This is part of the obligation undertaken when assuming positions of authority, and it requires a measure of moral courage. Not to speak when

---

14. See Covey, "Being Loyal to Those Not Present," in *8th Habit*, 174–75; and Covey, *Trust*, 168–69.

speaking is appropriate is to give silent assent to an abuse. It is true that pastoral prudence will sometimes suggest that an intervention be deferred or its tenor lightened, lest in scraping off the rust the vessel be holed (RB 64.11). This, however, is something quite different from doing almost nothing except to hope that the situation will somehow remedy itself. In such a case the silence is loudly shouting a message that drowns out many sessions of solid teaching or sound advice. The abbot, says Saint Benedict, "should not cover up the sins of those who commit crimes, but root them out as soon as they appear, while he is able" (RB 2.26). There is no point in verbally proclaiming virtue while allowing vice to flourish. This is true also in minor matters and not only in serious deviations from what is right.

Truth in speaking often requires truth in acting. This means that preachers have to practice and that those in authority in a monastery have to be careful about the promises they make. When a promise is made, that which was previously optional becomes obligatory. This is especially binding in the case of those who stand in Christ's place. We do not trust those who do not deliver on a promise. It means their word is unreliable. It follows that we should be careful about the promises and commitments we make to others so that, once they are made, we fulfill them without procrastination or prevarication. As a rule, people do not expect every request to be granted or every suggestion to be followed. What they want is to be heard without defensiveness or aggression. And they expect an honest and timely response, even if it goes against what they had hoped.

As a junior, I asked permission of my abbot to move my small work department into some free space. The response was, "I will think about it and get back to you." The following week, when I inquired as to the progress of the decision making, I was shooed away with, "I will let you know when I have made up my mind." About twenty years later, as we both watched the building in question being demolished, the abbot turned to me and said, "Well, you won't be moving in now, will you?" In the interim I had realized that there were good reasons against the move, but this did not reduce my frustration at not receiving an honest response. The lack of an answer damaged the relationship more than a refusal would have. This disenchantment is similar to what Friedrich Nietzsche described in this way: "What upsets me is not that you lied to me, but that I can no longer believe you."[15]

To win or maintain trust often means actively responding to what we have heard from another. If we are in some official position, information laid at our door is meant to lead to some sort of action or at least to an explanation of why inaction is preferable at this moment. We cannot ignore such data or concentrate solely on the subjective state of the informant. The purpose of the communication is to generate a response. In every community there are people who get things done, and it is to these that we turn when something needs doing. We trust them. We do not really have much faith in those who merely talk or who conveniently forget anything that requires exertion. Forgetfulness has no part to play in sound pastoral strategy.

In a formation situation, the formator will often be confronted with criticisms or mockery of seniors who are not living in accordance with the newcomers' ideals. There is a temptation to respond defensively or with a counteraccusation. Often the criticism comes from a failure to understand a complex situation and an overreadiness to cast the first stone. To respond truthfully means, on the one hand, explaining some of the less public elements of the situation without trying to whitewash the reality. On the other hand, it may mean—gently and at an appropriate time—exploring where the criticism is really coming from. The whole truth is most often the best defense.

6. *Acting Transparently*. Mistrust is generated when practical decisions are implemented without appropriate consultation, explanation, or preparation. Often a single person or a smaller

---

15. Quoted in Covey, *Trust*, 138.

group examines the options and makes a choice. Presupposing that the decision is a rational one, it is likely that the same conclusion would have been reached after a wider consultation. The difference is that if all had participated in the choice, it would be easier for all to own what was decided. Taking shortcuts may speed up the process, but it creates at least the semblance of autocracy, which, cumulatively, may nurture discontent and undermine trust. Imposing on ourselves a level of consultation and accountability beyond the minimum is a sure way of demonstrating to others that we can be trusted.

It is worth remembering that according to the third chapter of Saint Benedict's Rule, the most significant matters are to be referred to the whole community; lesser matters are to be referred to the counsel of the seniors only (RB 3.1, 12). The reverse is sometimes seen: anything really important is handled by the abbot's council or by a kitchen cabinet. Apart from those matters prescribed by law, only self-evident or relatively unimportant matters are thrown open to the community.

A good level of transparency ensures that there is equitable access to community resources and fairness in the allocation of onerous tasks. Lack of transparency generates suspicion and a sense of injustice and impotence for those members who consider themselves to be out of the loop. If participation in decision-making processes is an important and ongoing way of socializing members of a group, as Habermas suggests, then exclusion will almost certainly alienate. Empowerment builds trust, disempowerment erodes it.

The best way of receiving trust is to give it in abundance, to trust others, to delegate, to make room for them to develop talents as yet unseen. Saint Benedict's chapter on deans (RB 21) suggests an alternative to a purely vertical hierarchy. By dividing the community into groups of ten, each under the care of a person with delegated responsibility, a degree of subsidiarity was introduced, and there was the possibility of a general sense of participation in the day-to-day running of the community. A willingness to share power has a good effect on morale, but it has to be more than window-dressing. The key to successful delegation is the balance of rights and duties. There are no privileges without corresponding obligations, on the one hand, and, on the other, no duties without rights.

7. *Maintaining Confidentiality.* One of the inhibiting factors to transparency in a monastery is the need for confidentiality. Some matters that are discussed in the internal forum can influence practical decisions, but the reasons for these decisions cannot always be publicly revealed. This means that for those outside the circle, the decisions have to be taken on trust. I think everybody in a monastic community understands and accepts this. Confidentiality, however, needs to be weighed against the value of explaining the reasons behind particular decisions so as to win the "voluntary obedience" to which *Perfectae Caritatis* referred.[16] It should not be used as "national security" is sometimes used in civil society, that is, as a means of avoiding appropriate disclosure and as a cover-up for sloppy administration or incompetence.

Having a secure space in which to bare one's soul is one of the great benefits that monastic life offers. Such openness requires much trust. A zeal for confidentiality not only guarantees the freedom of conscience that canon law requires but protects the privacy of personal data. We do not necessarily want everyone to know everything about us, nor what we reveal to one to become known to all.

In a formation situation, formators often have to keep several alternative but overlapping narratives distinct. This is especially so when dealing with situations of conflict, suspicion, envy, or sexual attraction among those in their care. The same incident will probably be described differently by different people. There should be no leakage from one account to another. The formator needs to remain focused on the person who is speaking, trying to help that person to reframe the

---

16. *Perfectæ Caritatis*, 14; 346.

experience in a way that leads to greater self-understanding. For the moment this is more important that arbitrating differences, allocating blame, or solving problems. At a later time there may be scope for a facilitated meeting of the parties to settle differences openly and amicably, but meanwhile each narrative has to be heard on its own merits.

8. *Admitting Mistakes*. Warren Buffet once said, "It takes twenty years to build a reputation and five minutes to ruin it."[17] Beset as we all are with areas of ignorance, weakness, and maybe malice, it is impossible for us never to make mistakes and misjudgments in our dealings with others. Some of these are small matters in the world of objective outcomes, but they can loom large in the heightened sensitivity of those who rely on us for total support and who may have unrelenting and unrealistic expectations of us. Even in an ambience that preaches mutual forgiveness, a simple mistake or a moment of weakness may generate grievances that fester for years.

Sometimes what we have done or failed to do has a disproportionate effect. It can happen that crises of trust are engineered by others for ulterior motives and then spread like wildfire. They can be based on erroneous information or a hasty interpretation. They can be simply an indication that a mentoring relationship has reached its termination.[18] Usually there is no smoke without fire; whether intentionally or not, the offender

---

17. Quoted in Covey, *Trust*, 131.
18. "The termination of a close tie with a mentor . . . is often a mutually painful, tortuous process. A man in his late thirties is not only giving up his current mentor, he is outgrowing the readiness to be the protégé of any older person. He must reject the mentoring relationship not because it is intrinsically harmful but because it has served its purpose. . . . The relationship is made untenable by the yearning for the good father, the anxiety over the bad father, and the projection of both these internal figures onto the mentor, who is the one often caught in a bind." Daniel J. Levinson, *The Seasons of a Man's Life* (New York: Ballantine Books, 1978) 147.

has done something that would have been better left undone. The initial trigger may be quickly forgotten as supporting evidence is accumulated, and it may not much matter if there is an untruth at the heart of the crisis. Feelings once aroused are not easily soothed. A manufactured or magnified grievance has no less power to destroy trust than a justified complaint.

Words once spoken cannot be unsaid, nor deeds undone. A superior or formator caught in a situation like this has to engage in damage control. This means that aggression is not reciprocated, that hurt feelings and thoughts of vengeance do not play a part in the response, and that, where possible, counsel is sought. Since offense often causes withdrawal, bridges have to be built or rebuilt. The offended party must be sought out and a sincere apology offered. This must contain the rarely uttered words "I was wrong."[19] This initial contact may not be the best time to offer excuses or explanations. The important thing is that we feel remorse that an action or omission of ours has caused disturbance and distress in another. The apology is sincere. The casuistry can wait.

It is very useful to talk to a supervisor about how the incident has affected us because, in most cases, we have to pick ourselves up and go on with life. We do not have the luxury of withdrawing from all involvement, as the other party may. And we may never have the opportunity to express fully our side of the story. A quick remedy for the invisible wounds is not always possible even when overt reconciliation occurs and civility is restored. The situation will never return to its previous level of trust; it will either be better or worse. If it is better, it will be because an immature relationship has been replaced by something more adult and realistic.

---

19. "At one point in writing about the General Will, Jean-Jacques Rousseau said that, for democracy to work, citizens must be willing to say, 'I was mistaken.' This is not something most of us are willing to do." Andrew Hacker, "Twelve Angry Persons," *New York Review of Books* 42.14 (21 September 1995) 46.

The breakdown of a trusting relationship calls for resilience. Four skills are involved if we are to survive: we have to be robust enough not to lose heart but to keep going; we have to be resourceful in controlling the damage; we have to try to recover what has been lost; and we have to learn from our mistakes.[20]

It is in learning from our mistakes that we grow in wisdom and increase our dexterity in dealing with the sensitivities of other people.[21] Trust is impaired when, by our actions or omissions, we reveal defects in our pastoral competence or in our character. In itself, such a failure changes nothing; it merely unveils a weakness that was hidden. Apart from the pain caused, it can be welcomed as a moment of revelation and an invitation to begin to reform ourselves and to do what we do more effectively:

> Whether you lose the trust of others through a conscious act of betrayal, poor judgment, an honest mistake, a failure of competence, or a simple misunderstanding, the path to restoration is the same: to increase your personal credibility and behave in ways that inspire trust. If you've broken trust

---

20. Thus Stephen E. Flynn, "America the Resilient: Defying Terrorism and Mitigating Natural Disasters," *Foreign Affairs* 87.2 (2008) 6–7: "Such resilience results from sustained commitment to four factors. First, there is robustness, the ability to keep operating or to stay standing in the face of disaster. . . . Second is resourcefulness, which involves skilfully managing a disaster once it unfolds. . . . The third element of resilience is rapid recovery, which is the capacity to get things back to normal as quickly as possible after a disaster. . . . Finally, resilience means having the means to absorb the new lessons that can be drawn from a catastrophe."

21. Here is a description of what may be required: "Honda was immediately alert to Kiyoaki's lesson. He knew that to retain Kiyoaki's affection he must check the unthinking roughness that friendship ordinarily permitted. He had to treat him as warily as one would a freshly painted wall, on which the slightest careless touch would leave an indelible fingerprint. Should the circumstances demand it, he would have to go so far as to pretend not to notice Kiyoaki's mortal agony." Yukio Mishima, *Spring Snow* (Tokyo: Charles E. Tuttle Company, 1972) 32.

with someone else, it's an opportunity to get your own act together, to improve your character and competence, to behave in ways that inspire trust. Hopefully this will influence the offended party to restore trust in you. But even if it doesn't, your effort may well affect others in positive ways, and it will definitely enable you to create more high-trust relationships in the future.[22]

Pastoral dealings with others are always challenging precisely because they are a constant reminder of our own deficiencies and an urgent prompting to remedy them. As Saint Benedict says of the abbot, "When he helps others to amend by his admonitions, the amendment of his own vices is brought about" (RB 2.40).

* * *

The way to begin a culture of mutual trust and mutual fidelity is to work to increase one's own level of trustworthiness. For this a high degree of self-knowledge is necessary, together with a willingness to keep working to reduce one's personal liabilities. Complacency and slackness regarding one's own life will be taken as an indication of general untrustworthiness in dealing with others. In addition, to build trust we have to be prepared generously to trust others, and to do this we have to have a solid degree of self-confidence; insecurity makes us hesitant to believe in the good will and competence of those around us. The whole area of trust is fraught with risk, but to the extent that it is successfully negotiated, it yields abundant benefits for all concerned. And it is only in an ambience of mutual trust that real formation occurs.

---

22. Covey, *Trust*, 303, 315.

Chapter Eight

THE FORMATIVE CONVERSATION

Formative conversation is the principal means by which the monastic *conversatio* becomes formative. This is stated clearly by the thirteenth-century Cistercian Adam of Perseigne, who advocates "friendly and frequent conversation [*collocutio*] on spiritual matters or on the regular observance" among his favored means of formation.[1] Such conversations, whether formal or casual, are not limited to exchanges with the formator; the same benefit can also flow, as we have already remarked, from serious and adult conversation with other members of the community.

There are many overlapping levels in conversation, from small talk to deep interpersonal communion. At the right time and place they are all helpful. They all require a certain attentiveness and discipline if they are to bear fruit:

> Many persons fail in conversation because they so enjoy talking that they cannot bear to listen. . . . Conversation is not a lecture, a performance, a diatribe, a sermon, a negotiation, a cross-examination, a confession, a challenge, a display of learning, an oral history, or a proclamation of personal opinion.[2]

---

1. Adam of Perseigne, *Letter* 5:55; SChr 66, 118. See *The Letters of Adam of Perseigne* (Kalamazoo, MI: Cistercian Publications, 1976) 103. In his introduction to this volume, under the title "Monastic Formation according to Adam of Perseigne," Thomas Merton comments on this passage: "The atmosphere of direction must then be one of unaffected simplicity and spontaneity, completely informal and even somewhat merry" (23).

2. Russell Baker, "Talking It Up," *The New York Review of Books* 53.8 (11 May 2006) 4–5. The book under review was Stephen Miller's *Conversation: A History of a Declining Art* (New Haven, CT: Yale University Press, 2006).

The principal channel by which general formation is integrated and given focus is the regular interview, whatever it is called, in which the formator meets face to face with the novice or junior. The formator's principal task at this time is to listen and to hear both what is said and what is left unsaid. With different persons different techniques will be needed. With some there is a flood of words that will have to be slowed down, with others a tendency to wander away from the point will need to be checked, and with others there will be long silences while the apparent inability to say anything at all is faced.

Intensive listening is not merely passive. It is the formator's responsibility to ensure that the thread of self-disclosure does not become so tangled that both speaker and listener become lost. This involves continual checking back to make sure that what is being heard is the same as what is being intended. The formator can never be sure of this until some verification is given by the other person. This is most easily done by paraphrasing at an appropriate point what has been said and giving it a focus. "When you said you were disturbed, did you mean that you were angry?" The response might be, "Yes, very angry indeed!" or "No, not angry but just upset and a little bit depressed." In both cases the clarification has added some content not previously included. It is important to make sure that no approval or disapproval is communicated at what is said. The formator's body language and tone of voice can easily give a subtle signal that what has been raised is not a suitable topic for discussion. If, for example, the formator becomes tense the moment sexual issues are mentioned, it is likely that the other person will veer away from the topic. The formator should try to reflect back to the person in a neutral tone what has been heard. The echo from the formator pauses the progression of self-disclosure for a moment and often allows the discourse to drop down to a deeper level. If a real empathy exists, the person speaking may scarcely notice the interruption.

Part of the dynamic of this kind of interview is that it establishes a common vocabulary in which issues may be discussed. This is particularly important in the area of sexuality, where some neutral ground has to be found between what is excessively clinical, on the one hand, and what is vulgar and verging on the obscene, on the other. More generally, many persons (men especially), even among those who have been well educated, are emotionally illiterate; they cannot read their own feelings. They do not appreciate that there is another dimension of perception and description beyond the merely factual and scientific. Being able to be aware of one's feelings, to read them well, and to describe them accurately is an important factor in human happiness.[3] Even more widespread is the incapacity to recognize and identify what is happening spiritually. Spiritual literacy is equally vital for any who choose to give priority to the spiritual life. This involves the ancient monastic art of discernment: *diakrisis*, *discretio*. Being able to name what one has felt is a key factor in being able to reframe experience within the context of a broader tradition. So, one arrives at the point of being able to say, "This is 'desire for God,'" "this is 'compunction,'" or "this is the 'dark night of the soul.'"

Nothing is excluded from the content of these conversations, but the formator needs to steer the flow of talk so that the other is speaking about his or her concrete experience of monastic life—the inner face of participation in the life of the community. Commentary on the lives of others should be tweaked to become descriptive of self. Nothing should be allowed to pass without reflection. There should be equal attention paid to positive and negative experiences so that the formator does not appear to be more interested in one than in the other. This would be subtly to reward one kind of experience and to punish the other. Applauding the overcoming of a bad habit may give the impression that the formator's approval is dependent on such victories. Thereafter, there may be a tendency to speak less about failures or to push them

---

3. See Daniel Goleman, *Emotional Intelligence: Why It Can Matter More than IQ* (London: Bloomsbury, 1996).

away by rationalization and denial. The speaker needs to feel free to raise any topic at all, no matter how unwelcome. This includes speaking about a general discomfort in monastic life or about a particular unease in dealing with the formator. "If your talented people are not happy, you have to find out why."[4] Feeling uncomfortable is the first step in breaking up a relationship, and the feeling grows stronger when it is kept secret.[5] If it is revealed, it may be possible to do something about reducing its causes, while if it is hidden, its influence grows. As the English poet William Blake wrote in "A Poison Tree,"

> I was angry with my friend:
> I told my wrath, my wrath did end.
> I was angry with my foe:
> I told it not, my wrath did grow.

It is clear that the method, if not the purpose, of this kind of interview is essentially nondirective. This will often mean that one refrains from offering advice in order to permit the other person eventually to come to the same conclusion through reflection and experience.[6] What is sought is a growth in self-knowledge and, beyond that, an ongoing growth in self-acceptance. Self-acceptance is often the product of empathetic listening. When another person hears my story and seems

---

4. Benjamin Chaminade, as quoted in *The Bulletin*, 10 August 2005, 66.

5. "Uncoupling begins with a secret. One of the partners starts to feel uncomfortable in the relationship." Diane Vaughan, *Uncoupling: How and Why Relationships Fall Apart* (London: Methuen, 1987) 11.

6. "Real teaching demands energy as well. To instruct calls for energy, and to remain almost silent, but watchful and helpful, while students instruct themselves, calls for even greater energy. To see someone fall (which will teach him not to fall again) when a word from you would keep him on his feet but ignorant of an important danger, is one of the tasks of a teacher that calls for special energy, because holding in is more demanding than crying out." Robertson Davies, *The Rebel Angels* (Harmondsworth: Penguin Books, 1981) 92.

undismayed by its negativities and does not rush in to remedy them, I am encouraged to go deeper, somewhat confident that what I find will not be so terrible. Long before the topic of better behavior comes to the forefront of discussion, it is necessary to spend much time combating the waves of self-doubt and self-rejection that assail many people, at least occasionally. If a point of behavior that needs attention comes up, it may be advisable in some circumstances to say, "Yes, that is something that needs to be done. Let's talk about it later in the year." Concentrating on fixing problems may divert attention from the more important task of understanding where they come from. Furthermore, our enthusiasm to reduce negative behavior may give the message that our acceptance of the other is somehow conditional. These interviews should not become problem-fixing sessions. As soon as we switch to the problem-solving mode, our attention is divided, listening is impaired, we catch less of the data being offered to us, and as a result our hasty "solutions" are based on incomplete data. Meanwhile, the other person quickly realizes that we are no longer fully with them, and the flow of conversation falters. Now is the time for listening; later we can make executive decisions about what to do.

These interviews are to be considered long-term, probably lasting at least a couple of years. It is important first to listen well without attempting to push the person in a particular direction. This is the art of accompaniment about which much has been written in recent years.[7] Time is needed to create an environment hospitable to self-revelation. Often the conversations circle around the same points, spiraling closer to the heart of the matter. This especially requires patient attention, waiting to pick up the previously unmentioned clue that opens the door to a richer space within.

---

7. See, in particular, André Louf, *Grace Can Do More: Spiritual Accompani-ment and Spiritual Growth* (Kalamazoo, MI: Cistercian Publications, 2002).

On a practical level, if the person's self-disclosure is taken seriously, the formator will be diligent in not allowing any part of it to go unnoticed. Often it is an outsider who is able to put the pieces of a person's story side by side and show their connection. Each part of the narrative needs to be slotted in with the emerging whole and not treated as though it were unconnected from the rest of the story. Depending on the formator's memory, more or less detailed notes will need to be written up after the interview, along with the formator's unasked questions and points that need to be brought up again at a later stage. These notes will form the basis of the formator's ongoing reflection and immediate preparation for the next meeting. The more thoughtful and prayerful preparation is invested, the more spontaneous and freely flowing the encounter will be.

The key skill on which formators need to rely is empathy, a respectful understanding of what another is experiencing. This is a quality genetically more often associated with females than with males.[8] The problem is that we rarely know when we are lacking in empathy because, like color blindness, the defect is an insensitivity of which we are unaware. We do not know what we are missing. Empathy is a natural quality in human beings rather than a skill that can be acquired; it can, however, be allowed to develop.

---

8. Baron-Cohen, *The Essential Difference: The Truth about the Male and Female Brain* (New York: Basic Books, 2003) 2–3, 29–60. See also 101: "Lower levels of fetal testosterone (seen more commonly in females) lead to better levels of language, communications skills, eye contact, and social skills—all signs of better empathizing. And if restricted interests are an indicator of in-depth systemizing, these results clearly show that good systemizing abilities are linked to higher levels of fetal testosterone." Fetal testosterone levels are indicated by the length of the ring finger relative to the index finger. See Ridley, *Nature via Nurture*, 157. This innate difference may explain why men often feel more comfortable in the exercise of effective love rather than in feelings of affective love.

The best way to make room for empathy to blossom is to put aside egotistic concerns in order to pay attention to the other. Included among these concerns is the desire to be a successful empathizer! The formator needs to keep saying, "This is not about me." Chuang Tzu, a Chinese sage, expressed this necessity for emptiness thus:

> The hearing that is only in the ears is one thing. The hearing of the understanding is another. But the hearing of the spirit is not limited to any one faculty, to the ear or to the mind. Hence it demands the emptiness of all the faculties. And when the faculties are empty, then the whole being listens. There is then a direct grasp of what is right there before you that can never be heard with the ear or understood with the mind.[9]

Deep conversation requires an asceticism by which self-assertion is reduced. To hear what others are attempting to communicate requires that we put aside our own agenda and concentrate on the other person as if no one else existed in the universe and as if nothing were so important to us as hearing what the other person wishes to communicate. This is where the fact that a formator often has multiple roles makes perfect listening difficult. A work assignment to be discussed, a dispute to be resolved, a correction to be given, and any other necessary intervention fill the formator's memory and clamor for attention. At this time and in this situation they must be ignored.

It is also important to recognize different kinds of communication in what others say to us. We have to be on their wavelength. The simple statement "It was cold this morning" may be a meteorological remark that requires a similar response: "Yes, and more cold weather is expected." Or it may

---

9. This point is developed, together with the quotation from Chuang Tzu, in Marshall B. Rosenberg, *Nonviolent Communication: A Language of Life* (Encinita, CA: PuddleDancer Press, 2003) 91–104.

be an indication of how the other person is feeling, so some sort of sympathy is needed: "You must have wished you were back in the tropics." Or it may be the expression of a physical or emotional need that requires an answer such as "Is your heater working OK?" or the comforting assurance "I know how hard winter is for you." Finally, it may be an implicit request that expects the formator to respond appropriately: "Do you need to buy some warm clothes?"

What we are doing in such responses is checking that we have picked up what the other was really trying to pass on to us in a banal statement about the weather. Each time we succeed, not only does our trust account increase but, more importantly, we increase our confidence in our ability to connect with the other person. This mood matching lays the foundation for deeper exchanges. It is a matter of "rejoicing with those who rejoice and grieving with those who grieve" (Rom 12:15). We deliberately leave aside our own mood in order to enter that of the person with whom we are speaking.

It is this leaving aside of self in order to be attentive to others that will, in the long term, make our conversations formative:

> Empathy makes real communication possible. Talking *at* a person is not real communication. It is monologue. If you talk for significantly more than 50 percent of the time every few sentences, it is not a conversation. It is venting, or storytelling, or lecturing, or indoctrinating, or controlling, or persuading, or dominating, or filling silence. In any conversation there is a risk that one party will hijack the topic in an undemocratic manner. He may not intend to be undemocratic, but in hijacking the conversation the speaker does not stop to consider that, if he is doing all the talking, this is only fulfilling *his* needs, not the listener's. Empathy ensures this risk is minimized by enabling the speaker to check how long to carry on, as well as to be receptive to the listener's wish to switch to a different topic. Real conversation is sensitive to *this* listener at *this* time. Empathy leads you to ask the listener how *she* feels, to check if *she* wants to

enter the dialogue, or to see what *she* thinks about the topic. But you do not check once and then ignore her thoughts and feelings while you focus on your own. Rather, you keep asking, frequently, in the course of the dialogue.[10]

Empathy sometimes takes us to places we would rather not enter. If we have been tested and found true, the person to whom we are speaking may make the decision to share with us the shame that has been a burden for many years. Shame is not exactly the same as guilt, though the two often overlap. The source of this shame need not be moral. Guilt is the remorse and self-condemnation that results from a bad action. It is a judgment on what was done. Shame concerns who and what we are. It is a deep negativity that makes any further foray into self-knowledge threatening and prevents any growth in self-acceptance. Shame undermines self-esteem.

Feelings of shame can come from a variety of sources. Every deviation from what is commonly considered "normal" engenders shame, whether the distinction is inherited, voluntary, or simply the result of an inadvertent solecism. Shame is what we feel when we are singled out as not belonging to a group or when we are excluded from it, whether publicly or in the secret recesses of our own feeling.[11] To cause shame

---

10. Baron-Cohen, *The Essential Difference*, 23.

11. Some cultures use shame as a means of social control. The Romans tattooed criminals; in medieval times the stocks and the pillories were used; in the American Civil War deserters were sometimes branded. In many criminal systems shame is still used both to punish the offender and to serve as a deterrent to others. Even before guilt is formally ascertained in court, the accused is made to run the gauntlet of television cameras—to be marked as an offender by millions of viewers, perhaps irrespective of the final verdict. See Martha C. Nussbaum, *Hiding from Humanity: Disgust, Shame and the Law* (Princeton, NJ: Princeton University Press, 2004) 217–50. Shame has also been used punitively by the Church. When those who are considered to be in a state of mortal sin are excluded from receiving Holy Communion, they are marked out before the whole congregation as sinners—especially now that the Eucharistic

to another in a hitherto trusting relationship is usually a sign of a substantial lack or loss of empathy.[12]

Empathy allows us to make contact with what is deepest in the other person. Being introduced to the shame of others will always be unexpected, and sometimes the exposure will come as a severe shock. The source of shame is generally hidden from the public gaze; it does not connect with what we know of the other's persona. The appropriate response is to demonstrate by body language, and maybe by what we say, that our regard for the other person is undiminished because it is unconditional. We need to remain calm and enter fully into the other's horror without trying to minimize it. It is not a matter of saying too quickly, "Don't worry about that," "That's nothing," or "I've often done the same thing myself." Nor is this the time to trump the revelation with a trite "spiritual" sentiment. The essential part of our response is to be with the other person, to be present quietly and without trepidation, absorbing some of the pain, not trying to find a facile solution and not attempting to shorten the moment and to pass on to something else. This may be the beginning of a long and pain-filled series of conversations that are not of the formator's choosing but, with God's grace, may be a source of comfort and healing to the other person.

Because the formator is human, sometimes these sessions will have a strong emotional impact, one that could almost be described as a mild form of posttraumatic stress. Absorbing the pain of others takes its toll. The sense of helplessness at the horror of an abusive situation, for example, can paralyze the formator or arouse a tangle of unhelpful and conflicting emotions. It is in such cases as these that the value of hav-

---

fast has been relaxed. Saint Benedict deliberately wishes to arouse shame (*verecundia*) in latecomers by having them stand apart from the community (RB 43.7); indeed, the whole process of excommunication can be viewed in this light.

12. See Neil Pembroke, *The Art of Listening: Dialogue, Shame and Pastoral Care* (Edinburgh: T&T Clark, 2002) 161–76.

ing a regular supervisor is most evident. A supervisor is not primarily a source of relevant information or an advisor on tactics but someone who helps us to process what we are feeling when we are helping others. When we recognize what is happening inside ourselves, our dealings with others are less likely to be influenced by our own interior turmoil. We will be sufficiently empty to listen well and to take our cue from what we are hearing and not from what we are feeling.

Reflection on our response to a particular difficulty will sometimes lead us to the conclusion that we are not the best person to be dealing with particular aspects of this situation. In that case our duty is one of referral. This is not always easy, since the other person may dread having to share the secret with another counselor and may feel secure with us. It is necessary, however, that we recognize the limits of our competence and steadfastly refuse to be drawn beyond them.

There is another area that can be fruitfully shared with a supervisor. Sometimes we feel badly treated by those in our care. Sometimes this may be because of an error or misjudgment on our part. More importantly, it may be because the other person refuses to confront a necessary challenge that it is our obligation to present to them. There is no guarantee that both parties will view the matter from the same perspective, and so time is needed after an intervention for some fusion of horizons to be achieved. For example, in an exceptional situation we may have to say, "If you continue to act in this manner, I cannot honestly recommend you for profession." If we assume that there is a basis for this statement, it may well be resisted. The novice or junior may resort to sullen silence, an adolescent tantrum, a personal attack, an appeal to a higher and presumed friendlier authority, or, if all else fails, detraction and rebellion. It is as though the formator is being punished for daring to speak out.

The area of correction is usually difficult for formators and is often raised at their meetings. How is it possible to maintain the trust of persons when they are unwilling to accept corrections, even when these are offered delicately and tentatively? It is no help to say that accepting feedback is an unavoidable aspect of adult existence. Those in formation are often extremely sensitive to any perceived criticism, especially when it comes from someone to whom they have opened their heart. At least part of this difficulty comes from a formator having to wear so many hats at once. One has to be, as Saint Benedict says of the abbot, "now a dire master and now a kind father" (RB 2.24). Perhaps this is a case where the various officials in the community should be encouraged (and trained) to speak out within their jurisdictions. A cantor may say, "You are singing too loudly." One in charge of a work department may point out that tools are being used carelessly. A teacher may correct a serial latecomer. This is to handle the problem on the spot and not allow the abuse to fester. The feedback needs to be tightly focused and well evidenced. It deals with a disruptive behavior; it should not be allowed to become a generalized criticism of the person.

A time will come when novices or juniors will pass out of the immediate care of a formator and be on their own. With this in mind, they should be trained in the art of autocorrection. This means having a well-formed conscience and taking counsel with it from time to time, perhaps speaking with a spiritual senior and allowing what is read in *lectio* to pass judgment on behavior. Lent, Advent, and the New Year can be occasions in which they might be encouraged to ask the formator—or, at least, to ask themselves—whether there is anything they could be doing to upgrade their lives.

We are all aware that, although those who enter monasteries are beautiful and inspiring people who sincerely seek God and who have left everything to follow Christ, the dross of sin and rebellion has not been completely expelled. They will soon find themselves engaged in that most fundamental of all monastic pursuits: fighting the demons they did not know they had. Sometimes we, as formators, are drawn into the fray. This can be a dangerous task since our intrusion is threatening to whatever subpersonal forces are operating. The hazards notwithstanding, it remains our task to name the demons and to encourage the other to disavow them. We can expect resistance and counterattack, and we will not always succeed in liberating the other person from the influences under which they make their life-denying choices. But it is our duty to try.

The duality about which Saint Paul wrote in the seventh chapter of the Epistle to the Romans is, I am led to believe, a universal experience:

> In each of us there is a "yes" and a "no," refusal and acceptance. Sometimes we want to refuse our possibilities because the path onto which they are leading us looks dangerous, threatening. We need someone who is prepared to push us onto the path, so to speak. . . . Most, if not all, people live with unacknowledged polarities. That is to say there are "sub-selves" which are disavowed because to recognise them is anxiety-producing. Growth toward psychological wholeness involves recognising these disowned selves and integrating them into the community of the Self.[13]

Sometimes when we are admitted as friends into another's subjectivity, we find ourselves engaged in accompanying them as they struggle with this inner duality. If we try to push them onto the path, as Pembroke suggests, it can only be from the inside, at their invitation—not in the manner of a bulldozer, but as a friend who adds another shoulder to the wheel. In the final analysis, however, if our efforts to help are unsuccessful or are rebuffed, we may not necessarily be blameworthy. Just as persons are able freely to resist grace, so they have the freedom to decline the offer of help, even when it is not to their advantage to do so.

There is a final and fundamental consideration that I would like to offer about formative conversation. It is the promise of Christ that where two gather in his name he is there as a third

---

13. Neil Pembroke, *The Art of Listening*, 6.

(Matt 18:20). We are not alone in our pastoral participation in this interaction; there is a mysterious presence of Christ and his Spirit, which elevates what is taking place to a higher plane. We take part in the conversation, representing Christ. To get to this place we have to undergo a conscious process of self-emptying, a *kenosis*. The Christ whom we make present to the other is not so much the Wisdom of God or the Power of God but one who is "meek and humble of heart." If I had to name a quality or grace that is the most significant in a formative conversation, *meekness* would be my choice. This denominates an iron-willed abstention from all self-assertion, an openness to whatever Providence allows, a willingness to welcome sinners, a giving of self without counting the cost. There will be times in which the conversation goes swimmingly and we are conscious of the working of grace in both parties. As with prayer, however, not all is consolation. Sometimes the encounter will generate a sense of unfocused dread for one or the other party, or of hostility, or of a massive dividing wall preventing any understanding. Here, as in prayer, we need to be still and stay with the darkness, realizing that there is, for the moment, more truth in it than in an abundance of light. This is a time to endure, but it is also a time to repent of one's own limitations that may have contributed to the obscurity. And it is an experience that should propel us to prayer.

Chapter Nine

TEACHING THE TRADITION

I have already spoken about the importance of the community establishing agencies by which newcomers are introduced to the monastic tradition and to the range of beliefs and values that undergird the everyday living of the monastic *conversatio*. The question I now wish to address concerns the method of initiating newcomers into the wealth of ancient monastic wisdom.

Adult Learners

If you search for images of a teacher in Microsoft Word, the result typically represents teaching as one larger person of presumed greater competence imparting knowledge or skill to others of presumed lesser competence. This is usually the case in schools and universities. In monasteries it may be the case, but not universally. Men and women are entering monastic life at a later age and at a later stage in their own education. Whether it is academic knowledge or life experience, they will almost certainly know much about which potential monastic educators may be ignorant.

It is important to respect the prior learning of monastic students, of whatever age they are. They do not come to us as blanks, as *tabulæ rasæ*. Some are highly qualified, but all bring with them a certain amount of expertise in some area or another. They will learn better if we try to build on their existing knowledge base rather than if we ignore it. This can be a challenge. For those who have been trained in the scientific method, precision, sequence, definition, and measurement are important, and they have a strong sense of causality: if A, then

B. This can make the transition to a more humanistic approach profoundly disorienting. They need help in appreciating the specific method used in monastic studies in order to make the transition. For the moment, suffice it to say, we treat our students as adults; we respect what they have so far learned. This mode of educating adults is sometimes termed "andragogy" as distinct from pedagogy, the education of children.[1]

In general, adults want to be actively involved in their own education. The "jug-and-mug" approach, which reduces students to mere passive recipients, is not suitable. There will be times for the presentation of material that is new to them, but these need to be followed by periods during which the material is processed and the content validated from their own experience, applied to real life, and reexpressed within the context of their own beliefs and values.[2] Respectful exchanges within a group will usually help in coming to terms with what has been presented. The giving of assignments in which the students can, in a disciplined way, follow their own interests in researching a topic and writing it up can be a more potent learning experience than simply listening to someone else speak—no matter how qualified that person may be.

Although educational objectives need to be defined, a plurality of ways of meeting these objectives can be countenanced. While keeping within the basic flow of a subject, there is scope for some measure of heuristic learning in which students are encouraged to expand their knowledge of a topic by pursuing aspects of it that particularly arouse their interest and enthusiasm and, in due course, by sharing them with the group.

---

1. See Alan Brown, *Valuing Skills: Recognition of Prior Learning* (North Melbourne: The Victorian Education Foundation, 1992).

2. In general, for every nominal hour of lecturing, two or three hours should be allowed for discussion, additional reading, and personal appropriation of the material. Time for private study of an appropriate duration should be allocated on the daily schedule.

It is helpful to give some thought to the learning environment, whether it accurately reflects the nature and the needs of the participants. A schoolroom setup may not appeal to men and women of mature years. This concern begins with the physical setting. Purgatorial chairs do not make for good learning. Juggling books and writing materials is both a distraction and an excuse for opting out of full involvement. Temperature, light, and noiselessness need to be considered. The emotional ambience is also important, especially since what happens outside the sessions often interferes with what happens inside them. Noncontentious discussion reflecting different viewpoints should be welcomed, with some thought given to securing the confidentiality of the exchange.

In monasteries, where the students are few and the levels of education can be varied, a person-centered approach is possible. The objectives of a course can be redefined to suit this particular group and these particular individuals, with their unique range of skills and liabilities. The ambition is to expand the knowledge they already have, at whatever point in the spectrum they are, and to motivate them to keep expanding that knowledge when formal monastic education terminates. Thus, let them "moderate everything so that the strong will have something to desire and the weak will not run away" (RB 64.19).

I have found the approach of Parker Palmer helpful in a monastic setting. He speaks of a class as being a community of truth in which no one person has a monopoly on expertise. All are learners, patiently acquiring knowledge and wisdom from the "great thing" that is the object of their study and from one another.[3] The teacher is there as a guide into the tradition. This work may be done through several simultaneous channels: through explaining texts and contexts in a user-friendly manner, through encouraging interactive dialogue with the

---

3. Parker J. Palmer, *The Courage to Teach: Exploring the Inner Landscape of a Teacher's Life* (San Francisco: Jossey-Bass, 1998) 106–10.

text, through building bridges with experience, and through promoting heuristic learning. The paramount objectives are to give the students easy access to the tradition and an appreciation of its richness; they will have the rest of their lives to continue to be formed by the vast sea of traditional wisdom.

There will be those who grumble that they did not come into the monastery to study. Alternatively, there may be others who are in a hurry to tackle "real" studies that will better equip them for professional or priestly careers. A teacher or formator has to be prepared to give an answer to their questions. Depending on the underlying content of the query, some of the following points may be worth offering for consideration.

1. Organized study is a way of enhancing our *personal discipline*. It teaches us to work to a schedule, to observe priorities, and to meet deadlines. Through our sessions together we learn to go beyond subjective thinking, to listen respectfully to the viewpoints of others, and to appropriately modify our opinions so that they are more fully based on objective evidence.

2. Going beyond the elementary stage of monastic or theological knowledge is helpful in bringing about a certain *refinement of mind*; it initiates us into the language in which spiritual experience is described and thus enables us to bring to the surface deep questions that would otherwise have been beyond our powers of expression. In this way what we study contributes to the effectiveness of any spiritual direction we might receive and, in due course, will help us to help others verbalize their experiences. Studies can also contribute in raising newcomers to the general cultural level of the community.

3. Participating in a class situation is a way to engage in *serious conversation* about important matters, both with monastic contemporaries and with the seniors who are appointed as teachers. In this way we come to know better what other members of the community think about certain things, where they are coming from, and what their particular values are.

4. Monastic education programs prepare us for an *unknown future*. In the early years of monastic life nobody knows what is ahead of them, but it is certain that the better the foundation, the more stable will be what is built upon it. I have known men and women appointed to be formators or superiors who have lamented the fact that they were not themselves better initiated into the monastic tradition that they are now responsible for transmitting to others, whether this was the result of their own choices or because their community lacked resources.[4] The broader the base, the higher the structure can rise.

Monastic education is not the whole of formation, but it is a significant part and a valuable complement both to the intimacy of personal accompaniment and to the public immersion in the usual activities of the community.

Monastic Theology

There is a monastic approach to study that is distinct from the manner in which studies are done in universities. This

---

4. I came across the following paragraph many years ago, but unfortunately I have mislaid the reference. "The major sermon to the students will be this: *you do not have the moral option to choose not to learn*. Choosing not to learn is choosing not to know what you will need to know in order to make a contribution to the world. Your chosen ignorance may be the occasion of an accident, the loss of life, the failure of an important project, the frustration of a community's dream or the disappointment of people who were counting on you to perform. An organisation's or a community's achievement of excellence is dependent not only on the quality of its most talented members, but upon the intelligent co-operation of its ordinary members like you. The shoddy or incompetent work of anyone diminishes the achievement of the whole. As a civilisation, we have achieved whatever level of greatness, whatever level of excellence and whatever level of good order because countless people like you knew what to do when it counted most. They were prepared. That is why learning what you learn in school is not only a privilege; it is a duty to yourselves and to your community and to your future children and grandchildren."

concerns not only the matter of study and the methods of teaching and learning but also the subjective attitudes in which study is approached. The term "monastic theology" was devised by Jean Leclercq as a way of distinguishing the mode of discourse about God in medieval monasteries from that emerging in the schools of the period. In the monasteries, "theology" was not cultivated as a means of reaching objective conclusions so much as for the subjective enrichment of those who studied it; its aim was to contribute to a more complete living of the Gospel. Monastic theology was, to use an anachronism, existential. It was meant not only to be known but to be lived. Speaking of the apostles Peter and Paul as teachers, Saint Bernard writes:

> These are our masters who had learned the ways of life more fully from the Master himself and who continue to teach us right up to today. What did the holy Apostles teach us in the past and still teach us? They did not teach us the art of fishing or tent making or anything like that. They did not teach us to read Plato or to be occupied with the subtleties of Aristotle, to be always learning and never come to the knowledge of the truth. They taught me how to live.[5]

It is not that men such as Bernard of Clairvaux, William of Saint Thierry, and Isaac of Stella and, in the next century, women such as Gertrude of Helfta and Beatrice of Nazareth were incapable of pursuing academic studies or excelling in them. This was a deliberate choice of wisdom over knowledge. They chose to continue the patristic modes of reflection using the methods of rhetoric rather than to opt into the Aristotelian dialectics that was then beginning to shape what came to be called scholastic theology.

We cannot, of course, emigrate to the twelfth century, and there is no escaping the fact that both the content and the

---

5. Bernard of Clairvaux, PP 1:3; SBO 5, 189–90.

methods of theological discourse have become considerably more complex today. If, however, we are considering the study of theology (using this word in its broadest connotation) in terms of its formative function, then we can learn something from the medieval approach. This is not to dispute the value of rigorous systematic theology but to make the point that a different style of theological reflection and discourse is more powerful in communicating and strengthening the beliefs and values that undergird the monastic *conversatio*. This means in effect making a distinction and a separation between the study that is undertaken as a necessary part of monastic formation and that which will later equip the brother or sister for the ministries to which he or she will be assigned. It has to be said that, in these times of reduced personnel, there is a temptation to merge monastic and seminary studies with a view to producing priests as quickly as possible. This can easily result in a defective monastic formation, the fruits of which may not appear for several years.

There are three distinct levels in which monastic theology needs to flourish for a community to be able confidently to celebrate its identity. Most important is a general culture in which all or most of the members of the community appreciate monastic tradition and have recourse to it sometimes, not only in reading modern books about monastic spirituality but also in having some facility in reading the primary sources. There is a second, more developed level in which some can act as teachers and animators of upcoming monastic generations, giving them a basic understanding of the tradition and an appreciation of its value. Finally, there is a more specialized level, reserved for a few, in which research into monastic tradition becomes an important part of their lives' work. The fact that some are engaged professionally in monastic theology is not to be seen as an indication that it is desirable for all to be thus occupied. On the contrary, the quintessential expression of genuine monastic theology is not arcane scholarship but the simple existential reading of monastic texts as a spur to prayer and "to some degree of right living and the beginnings of monasticity" (RB 73.1).

Here are some of the characteristics of "monastic theology" that may find a resonance in the hearts of those who enter monastic life and that correspond to what they need at this stage of their lives.[6]

1. Monastic theology may be seen as *right-brain theology* and, as such, complementary to the left-brain theology of academic exploration. It is synthetic rather than analytic, with a touch of lyric poetry in its expression. It does not reduce complicated doctrines to theses or syllogisms but is happy enough to leave them in their partly unresolved state, since it does not strive to master its topic but to serve it, to admire it, to be filled with wonder at its beauty.[7]

2. Monastic theology is *experiential*. It invites readers to reflect on their own experience and to find the key to interpreting it in the Scriptures and in the writings of the ancient spiritual masters. Their reading is intended to cast its light on their daily lives and to invite them to repentance and conversion. It is not simply a source of knowledge; it aims at evangelization and reformation. Immersing oneself in the texts of monastic tradition is not only an introduction to monastic culture; it is also and primarily a pathway to self-awareness and self-knowledge. As Saint Athanasius wrote, "The Psalms are, for those who recite them, a mirror in which may be viewed the movements of the soul."[8] Many later treatises used the

---

6. See M. Casey, "'Emotionally Hollow, Esthetically Meaningless and Spiritually Empty': An Inquiry into Theological Discourse," *Colloquium* 14.1 (1981) 54–61. The quotation in the title is from Robert Pirsig, *Zen and the Art of Motorcycle Maintenance* (London: Corgi Books, 1976) 110.

7. "We embrace *ambiguity* not because we are confused or inadequate but because we understand the inadequacy of our concepts to embrace the vastness of great things." Palmer, *Courage to Teach*, 107.

8. Athanasius of Alexandria, *Letter to Marcellinus*, 12.

idea of a mirror in their titles—not a microscope or a telescope but a mirror. Studious reading is not for gaining knowledge about the outside world so much as for learning a little about oneself.[9]

3. Monastic theology is *devotional* in intent. It follows Saint Anselm's formula, *credo ut intelligam*. It is a work of faith that seeks to expand and deepen its understanding. Approached in a spirit of reverence, it sometimes leads the young monk or nun to quiet prayer and will often bear fruit at other times. On the spectrum between ordinary reading and *lectio divina*, monastic study tends to be closer to *lectio*, even though sometimes it is more active in chasing up references and allusions and in engaging in questioning and finding answers. Monastic study is much more exciting and stimulating than pure *lectio*, but it draws from the same sources and, eventually, serves the same purposes.

Part of the renewal of monastic life today must include the effort to motivate the followers of Saint Benedict to be "lovers of learning" in the sense that they read, reflect, and perhaps write, not because they need to prepare for some particular work to which they are assigned but out of sheer delight in spending time engaged in the timeless pursuit of wisdom. I think this is particularly appropriate as people grow older, retire from active professions, perhaps, and—notionally at least—have more time on their hands.[10] The ability to do this depends, of course, on their having acquired at least some of the necessary skills in their youth and on their having maintained an interest in monastic tradition as the background of whatever else they were doing in midlife.

---

9. See Margot Schmidt, art. "Miroir," in DSp 10.2 (1979), cc. 1290–1303.
10. See Elkhonon Goldberg, *The Wisdom Paradox: How Your Mind Can Grow Stronger As Your Brain Grows Older* (New York: Gotham Books, 2005).

Reading Texts

Benedictine tradition is a literary tradition. Throughout the centuries its lifestyle, spirituality, and wisdom have been written down, preserved, and transmitted to future generations. Today, more than ever, these sources are more generally in readable editions, with critical and explanatory apparatuses and in translation. This means that any program of renewal that includes a "return to the sources" has ample material to facilitate an appreciative understanding of the charism.

Reading ancient texts is hard work: they are written in a foreign language, they derive from an alien culture, and they address concerns different from those that occupy us. We undertake this labor because we are part of a tradition, and we will not understand ourselves fully as monastic persons until we appreciate the tradition in which we stand. What we receive when we embrace the integrity of monastic life is not fully present to our consciousness; it needs to be excavated. Openness to tradition is a way to fuller self-knowledge. And it "includes the acknowledgment that I must accept some things that are against myself."[11] When I look into the mirror of tradition, I am able to compare what I am with what I aspire to be. I am called to conversion. It is interesting that in accounts of monastic reform, it is often the bleak realization that the present has fallen away from the ideals of the past that triggers the desire to do better.[12] Even today, contact with tradition can enable monks and nuns to leapfrog unhealthy local conventions to nourish their sense of vocation at purer sources.

---

11. Hans-Georg Gadamer, *Truth and Method* (London: Sheed and Ward, 1965) 325.

12. Thus the founders of Cîteaux determined that their previous way of life "fell short of their desire and purpose to observe the Rule they had professed," and so they sought a lifestyle in harmony with the tradition in which they recognized their own calling. *Exordium Cistercii* 1, in Chrysogonus Waddell, *Narrative and Legislative Texts from Early Cîteaux* (Cîteaux: Commentarii Cistercienses, 1999) 400.

Part of the role of monastic education is to introduce newcomers to the wealth of this life-giving tradition. Although there may be some initial utility in showing videos of the life of Saint Benedict and giving an overview of the highs and lows of monastic history, the core of candidates' exposure to the tradition must be introducing them to the great texts in which the wisdom of the past is manifest. I will briefly discuss texts suitable for this purpose in the next section. As a general principle, however, it makes sense to begin with more accessible texts that speak to their immediate situations and serve to acquaint them with the good sense and literary charm of these ancient authors.

The basic technique of monastic theology is reading ancient texts in the light of present reality.[13] It would be unwise to presume that because all newcomers are literate and some of them are highly educated, this is a skill that they have already acquired. To begin with, this form of reading is intensive rather than extensive. The prized skill of speed-reading is not helpful here. Furthermore, those who have spent a great deal of time on the Internet will have developed different skills that make steady, linear application to a text difficult. There will be habits to be unlearned. Nicholas Carr notes that this is impossible unless there is a determined effort to avoid distractedness:

> It is the very fact that book reading "understimulates the senses" that makes the activity so intellectually rewarding. By allowing us to filter out distractions, to quiet the problem-solving functions of the frontal lobes, deep reading becomes a form of deep thinking. The mind of the experienced book reader is a calm mind, not a buzzing one.[14]

---

13. See M. Casey, "The Book of Experience: The Western Monastic Art of *Lectio Divina*," *Eye of the Heart* 2 (2008) 5–32.

14. Nicholas Carr, *The Shallows: What the Internet Is Doing to Our Brains* (New York: W. W. Norton & Company, 2010) 123.

What is required, above all, is the knack of close reading. This is the conclusion of Allan Bloom:

> A line-by-line, word-by-word analysis must be undertaken. . . . The hardest thing of all is the simplest to formulate: every word must be understood. It is hard because the eye tends to skip over just those things which are the most shocking or most call into question our way of looking at things. . . . The argument or example that seems irrelevant, trivial or boring is precisely the one most likely to be a sign of what is outside one's framework and which it calls into question. One passes over such things unless one takes pencil and paper, outlines, counts, stops at everything and tries to wonder.[15]

Close reading emphasizes quality over quantity: it aims at a quiet, reflective passage through a text, providing the reader with the opportunity for an enriched consideration of the issues raised. It is the experience of at least some that close attention to each element of the text before them has been an effective antidote to a chronic tendency to drowsiness. The mental activity involved in scrutinizing each element, asking disciplined questions, and seeking solutions has been found sufficient to keep one's mind from wandering and one's eyelids from growing heavy. It is a way of maintaining concentration without losing alertness.

Sessions of group reading, reflecting, and commenting on important texts of the monastic tradition should not be regarded as a pretext for idleness on the part of the teacher or leader. To be able to lead a group to a successful interchange, as distinct from sitting back and letting the discussion develop randomly, requires as much preparation as a straight lecture. The teacher needs to preview the discussion so as to be ready to facilitate its movement in appropriate directions.

---

15. Allan Bloom, "The Study of Texts," in *Giants and Dwarfs: Essays 1960–1990* (New York: Simon and Schuster, 1990) 306–7.

Some preparation is needed also to be able to provide basic information about the text being read and to prevent time being wasted by the group seeking answers to elementary questions.[16] The same norm holds for group reading as it does for all teaching: teach what you know; do not attempt to teach what you do not know.

Group sessions should be held with the aim of developing the habit of private study among the students, so that when they come together each will have the possibility of having something worthwhile to exchange with the others. The proportion of three hours of private work to one hour of group work does not seem unreasonable to me. Part of the learning process for new monastics is to discover for themselves the resources that even the sparsest monastic library contains. For some who are more accustomed to researching via the Internet, this may pose a challenge. This is where it is important to be clear about the purpose of monastic study as distinct from academic study in helping persons develop a profound understanding of the beliefs and values of the life to which they are in the process of committing themselves. As Nicholas Carr commented in the text quoted earlier, "deep reading becomes a form of deep thinking."

Forming a Canon?

Inevitably the question is asked: What should new monastics be asked to read? I do not think a lengthy list of required readings is useful since it encourages skimming and often occasions a sigh of relief and a sense of freedom when the

---

16. "Despite the current concern with pedagogical technique, no teacher can succeed for long without a sound grounding in the subject he or she is teaching. The basic knowledge is crucial, because students will quickly 'suss' a teacher who does not know his or her stuff. 'Knowing your subject is really the beginning of discipline,' an experienced teacher told me. 'Kids are like dogs; they know if you are uncertain.'" Jenny Stewart, "In Praise of Teaching," *Eureka Street* 16.3 (May–June 2006) 36.

obligation has been fulfilled. Formators will, over time, develop a sense of what is useful for newcomers to read in the context of their own community. With experience they will also have an idea of the order in which texts should be read. It makes sense to begin with shorter texts and extracts and then gradually move onto other texts that demand more application and that, with practice, will help students to develop the requisite skills. Finally, novices should arrive at the point of reading whole books from beginning to end and taking from them what speaks to their present experience, expanding their horizons, and, it must be admitted, occasionally learning to tolerate long, boring passages when the relevance of the text seems to have evaporated.

For all, the Rule of Saint Benedict is an obvious starting point. In the process of exploring the Rule, it becomes possible, as Benedict himself recommends in chapter 73, to expand the focus so as to take in some of Benedict's sources and, thus, introduce newcomers to the Desert Fathers and Mothers, to John Cassian, to Evagrius, to Augustine, and so forth. Thus the foundations are laid for a lifetime experience of reading the Rule in all the richness of its monastic context. As a semilegislative document, the Rule is fairly arid unless it is broken open by careful analysis and fertilized, as it were, by more luscious texts from the sort of reading that had formed Benedict's own attitudes.

Formal classes are not the only means of contact with the tradition; some information can be conveyed through readings in the refectory, as well as through exposure to monastic texts in the readings of the liturgy. And, in most places, the Rule is read continuously.

As a Cistercian, I am especially aware of the formative value of the writings of the great Cistercian authors of the twelfth and thirteenth centuries, which elaborate a spirituality based on the lifestyle of the Benedictine Rule but add to it three areas of emphasis that were of particular interest to their own contemporaries: an appreciation of the role of spiritual experience;

a recognition of the role of affectivity and the importance of making the monastery a *schola dilectionis*, a school of love; and giving due attention to the contemplative and mystical dimensions of monastic life. These qualities are of great importance also in our own times, and the early Cistercians can serve as a bridge between these contemporary aspirations and the older monastic traditions in which they are not always so obvious.

The temptation for Cistercians (at least) is to stop at what they consider to be the end of the golden age. This is understandable, but it is not so helpful. There is a certain value to be had in coming to appreciate the vicissitudes through which monasticism has passed in later times and the way that monasticism has attempted to retain its identity and character in a changing world marked successively by scholasticism, depopulation by plague and warfare, Reformation and Counter-Reformation, the Enlightenment, revolution, and secularization. We must resist the temptation of what Rembert Weakland called "neo-primitivism." The study of history and the reading of texts from all centuries have a cautionary function. By understanding how some lost fervor and became disoriented and how others kept afloat in difficult times, we may be inspired to keep alive the tradition we have received and to hand it on to others. We are, after all, heirs to a living tradition in its entirety, not self-styled reincarnations of a single part of that tradition. Right now we may not appreciate the value of all that we have received, but if we keep enlarging our capacity, we will eventually come to recognize the rich wisdom it conveys.

Chapter Ten

CRITERIA FOR CONTINUANCE

Saint Benedict regarded the novitiate as a time of systematic probation with the function of making sure that the candidates understand well the kind of life to which they are committing themselves and trying to confirm that they have the will to persevere in the *dura et aspera* of the monastic journey. At several points, as the candidates pass through the various stages of initiation, discernment will be needed. A practical judgment is to be made. It is never infallible and we cannot expect total certainty. It is possible, however, to isolate a number of areas where substantial evidence may be sought and found that a person really has a monastic vocation.

Before the temporally professed member of the community is admitted to solemn profession, there is a major period of discernment. As with entry, the issue divides into two fundamental questions. Is the candidate *suitable* to take final vows? Is the candidate *ready* to take final vows? These basic fields of investigation can be further subdivided. That so many questions are asked is an indication of the seriousness of the step confronting one about to make final profession. They can also serve as indicators of what sort of inner work needs to be done during the preceding period of formation.

This assessment needs to be done with great sensitivity since those asking for profession are in a position of great vulnerability. During the years of formation they have progressed in self-knowledge and have learned not to conceal their liabilities. Despite their best efforts, vices and inconsistencies remain, as they do with everyone. When they present themselves for solemn profession, they are fearful that too little will be made of their progress and too much of how far short they fall of absolute perfection. They are often a little resentful since, in their perspective, there may be some or many of the already professed who wear very lightly the monastic obligations that juniors are urged to ponder with so much gravity. Curiously, it can often seem that their severest critics are those whose own disorderly lives go unscrutinized.

Suitability

1. *Is there an evident commitment to all the practices constitutive of monastic* conversatio? Only those willing and able to embrace the integrity of monastic observance should be considered for solemn profession. In most cases, arriving at the point of asking for solemn profession will have involved a real struggle to overcome self in one area or another. The challenge may, for example, have occurred publicly in work, study, separation from family, solo singing, or community relations. Two areas of special attention, already flagged by Saint Benedict, are dedication to the Liturgy of the Hours and obedience. Sometimes the difficulty may have been more interior and obvious only in its effects, and it may be known to the formator only in the internal forum. A measure of victory in rising to the level of normality is a good sign. Struggles are not necessarily a bad sign. The overcoming of limitations in one area is an indication that growth is taking place, and it gives ground for the hope that it will continue and that other problem areas will eventually find resolution. Such candidates are not merely nesting in the monastery but working hard to go beyond their comfort zones and to permit themselves to be formed by the way of life they have embraced. It is to be hoped that the result of this settling into the monastic lifestyle is a deep sense of contentment that occasional reverses cannot displace. This is usually manifested by a general disposition of cheerfulness and generosity without excessive rigidity or fearfulness. Without such a joyous freedom, motivation for proceeding to solemn profession may be suspect.

2. *Has there been a solid investment in the practices of* lectio divina *and prayer?* This basic question concerns time set aside for personal communion with God. Unless substantial time is regularly given to prayer, the real challenges of prayer do not come to consciousness. In a general way, this concerns fidelity and assiduity to the personal practice of prayer in all its forms. Then we need to reflect on the quality of time thus spent. In normal circumstances a certain development will have been noted during the years of formation. Prayer normally becomes less florid, simpler, and much drier, driven by a more secret desire. Sentiment is slowly replaced by a will-based devotion that manifests itself by a willingness to spend time at prayer even though the experience is usually without dramatic impact. The cumulative effect of this fidelity is, however, readily discernible in behavior. What is being sought in the candidate is a growing taste for the hidden manna of contemplation, at least in its early stages, a contentment with a dry, unexciting prayer, and a willingness to spend time at it:

> Contemplative prayer is, in a way, simply the preference for the desert, for emptiness, for poverty. One has begun to know the meaning of contemplation when [one] intuitively and spontaneously seeks the dark and unknown path of aridity in preference to every other way. The contemplative is one who would rather not know than know. Rather not enjoy than enjoy. Rather not have *proof* that God loves him.[1]

With some persons the so-called dark night of the senses may occur during their time in formation. This may manifest itself not only in changes during the time of prayer but also in a generalized upheaval that affects many areas of their lives and may cause a vocational crisis.[2]

---

1. Thomas Merton, *The Climate of Monastic Prayer,* CS 1 (Spencer, MA: Cistercian Publications, 1970) 121.
2. See M. Casey, "The Deconstruction of Prayer," *Tjurunga* 51 (1996) 91–102.

Criteria for Continuance   167

3. *Is there a manifest capability of relating well to all members of the community?* This does not mean an equal degree of intimacy with all—that is unrealistic—but a capacity to communicate and cooperate with all, to live in harmony with all, plus a willingness to appreciate and enjoy the company of *everyone* in the community. Persons who are naturally introverted or shy may interact less boisterously than others. This is not to be confused with antisocial attitudes; it merely indicates a different pathway to the formation of good relationships. For such people, firm relationships may take longer to achieve but often run deeper. Living such relationships means having a capacity to tolerate differences, to forgive generously, and to be prepared to seek and receive forgiveness from others. A sure sign of being solidly implanted in the community is a progressive concern for the spiritual welfare of the community and of each of its members, as well as the willingness to exercise initiative and to take risks in doing what needs to be done to improve the current situation.

In the area of community relations, four particular behavior patterns need to be recognized as danger signals.

> i. *Selectivity in Relationship.* Where there are relationships between individuals that effectively (even though unintentionally) exclude others, trouble is brewing. Such long-term cliques of like-minded persons have a detrimental impact on community and do not augur well for the continuing growth of those involved. Those who enter a monastic community need to go beyond their natural boundaries to create solid affective links with all members of the community, excluding none. In particular, this means being able to relate in an adult way to the middle-aged: these are the people most actively involved in the administration of the various activities of the community and, hence, are the most likely to be targets of projections and criticisms. Sometimes persons can be very friendly with the aged, the marginal, and the young; these pose

no challenge to them and make no implicit demands on them. Meanwhile, they make little or no effort to accommodate those with a more dominant role in their regard or with a function in the administration of the community.

ii. *Extremes of Attachment and Detachment.* Sometimes a person develops a more intense relationship with one or other member of the community, either a contemporary or someone of a different age group or seniority. The relationship may be love or hate (in one of their numerous disguises), and it may be completely unilateral or somewhat reciprocal. There may be a more or less conscious sexual element involved in the attraction. In some cases the liaison can appear as codependency, each simultaneously feeding on and perpetuating the other's complementary needs. Together they create a kind of filter through which every other experience of community is interpreted and assessed.

iii. *Individualism.* More is involved here than the avoidance of eccentric and flamboyant behavior that does not concord with community style, although self-forgetfulness is a boon in any community.[3] Individualism is another name for selfishness. This is not only a feature of modern life; Baldwin of Forde noted this many centuries ago: "If someone lives only for himself and for his own advantage, and considers only himself in deciding how he should live, we can understand [this whole life] to be wholly dark."[4] Individualism is more than showing off; it is invading the space that properly belongs to others. There is also a quiet, passive form of individualism that consists in affective withdrawal from the community and the consequent downgrading of the significance of

---

3. See John Gallagher, "Individualism and Religious Life," *Review for Religious* 54.4 (1995) 585–88.

4. Baldwin of Forde, *Spiritual Tractates*, vol. 1, trans. David N. Bell (Kalamazoo, MI: Cistercian Publications, 1986) 169.

the community and its activities in the life of a particular person. This can be a hidden form of passive aggression. More obviously, the continual assertion of independence and entitlement can be a robust resistance to any form of reliance on others, a refusal to be put into a situation where favors or services must be asked or gratitude expressed. Interdependence is an essential component of community; without trustful mutuality, community is reduced to mere cohabitation. Genuine community includes not only the sharing of material goods; it also embraces a commonality of values.[5] If it is true that "pluralism means engagement with our differences,"[6] individualism undermines the development of authentic pluralism and tolerance because it is interested not in affirming or supporting others but only in throwing off any form of social constraint.

iv. *Narcissism.* Some of those who enter monasteries have learned from the ambient culture to demand that they be provided with all they need or want without question and without having to earn or repay anything. In the monastery their personal needs multiply beyond the common standards. There is a certain lack of enthusiasm for community tasks, even to the point of laziness. Often there will be the expectation that they will be allowed much space to do what they like. Failure to respond positively to such demands will often result in rages, tantrums, the drawing up of legalistic boundaries, the withdrawal of services, and sulking. All of these are tactics of avoidance; so long

---

5. John Paul II, *Veritatis Splendor,* 32: "There is a tendency to grant to the individual conscience the prerogative of independently determining the criteria of good and evil and then acting accordingly. Such an outlook is quite congenial to an individualist ethic, wherein each individual is faced with his own truth, different from the truth of others. Taken to its extreme consequences, this individualism leads to a denial of the very idea of human nature."

6. David L. Fleming, SJ, "Individualism in Community Life," *Human Development* 21:3 (2000) 8.

as rage continues, there is no possibility of engaging with reality. The best cure for narcissism is the cultivation of a sincere spirit of service. Those who enter a monastery to serve rather than to be served are constantly striving to increase their utility to the community and to other members, looking for new ways to displace self and give priority to the needs and even the desires of others. There are plenty of opportunities for this in most communities; those who are dedicated to serving others will find more fulfillment and happiness in community living than those whose universe revolves around themselves. Since their self-perceived needs are always increasing, narcissists will eventually arrive at a point where the community is unable or unwilling to accommodate their demands. At that point a crisis will ensue.

4. *Is there the capacity and desire to live the values of silence and solitude and to become strangers to worldly ways?* Those who do not accept the importance of moderation and even abstemiousness in speech, in the use of mass media, and in excursions and entertainment will be nuisances in the community for the rest of their lives, bridling at restrictions and undermining community discipline and morale. No matter what concessions are allowed, they will always be pushing the envelope further, sometimes stretching it to the breaking point. Here as elsewhere it is not so much a matter of having firmly defined and heavily policed boundaries as of ensuring that all the members of the community have internalized the specific monastic beliefs and values that call us to some degree of silence and solitude. Monastic values grow in solitary meditation and communal dialogue; if they are continually assailed by the voices of contrary philosophies, inevitably they will be eroded and contaminated.

5. *Has the person given positive signs of being receptive to monastic formation?* Before acceptance for solemn profession, there

needs to be positive evidence of a profound appreciation of the monastic patrimony and the willingness to safeguard its integrity. An important indicator of appropriate receptivity is the willingness to accept correction and, in a dialogical context, to change one's manner of living and acting as a result of it. More than slavish conformity to community norms and the directives of formators is needed to guarantee interior reception of formation; we look for signs that monastic values have been internalized. We hope that candidates will be able to live monastic life in a way not only concordant with common standards but expressive of a unique personality and call, as it were, in their own idiom. Without this marriage of inner and outer, external fidelity may be no more than pious sham, continued until final profession renders it unnecessary. A personal monastic style that is both original and, at the same time, faithful to the community's authentic tradition is usually an indication that formation has been effective. It is by being themselves that new members bring something fresh to the community, changing its basic composition and adding to its graced complexity.

6. *Is the person relatively free of inconsistencies?* Inconsistencies between the conscious, ideal self and the real self are, according to the conclusions drawn by the Jesuit psychologist Luigi Rulla, a major cause of nonperseverance in religious life. Inconsistency results when a need is stronger than the ideals—if the beliefs and values have not been internalized to the extent that they counteract the need. We are not always fully conscious of such needs or of the influence they exercise over our choices. One example of need is a deficiency: I need concrete expressions of love, attention, respect, affirmation, status, and comfort because I feel that I lack them, and without these my sense of self-worth is diminished. The urgent gratification of such a need may lead me to go against my fundamental beliefs and values. Another example is a giftedness that I need to exercise or develop: I need education, "outlets," and opportunities, otherwise I feel stunted in my growth,

frustrated, blocked; I am prepared to do almost anything to satisfy this need. This is how the team of psychologists from the Gregorian University sum up this situation:

> We are of the opinion that those individuals whose inconsistencies are unconscious or deeply preconscious are not changed much by new information; more exactly, the information they receive from the environment may influence them momentarily but not in the long run. These persons have defenses which prevent their becoming conscious of the true nature of their frustration, and which, as a result, make them incapable of modifying their behavior through a new evaluation or new learning. This inability to re-evaluate affects their vocation too; these individuals are unable to re-evaluate an unrealistic and unobjective self-ideal-in-situation.[7]

In some cases inconsistency causes an intractability that resists every effort formators make to break through. The problem is that although formators may intuit that all is not well, they may not always be aware of the extent to which there is inconsistency, especially when its expression occurs in the context of nonpublic activities. If it happens that the persons themselves have, by denial and repression, split off their inconsistent behavior from consciousness, uncovering the problem will be even more difficult. People with substantial areas of inconsistency should not be advanced to final profession.

Readiness

If a person appears to be suitable, the next question to be asked concerns their readiness to take the next step. In this matter it is not always possible to act as one would wish. There

---

7. Luigi M. Rulla, Franco Imoda, Joyce Ridick, *Psychological Structure and Vocation: A Study of the Motivations for Entering and Leaving the Religious Life* (Dublin: Villa Books, 1979) 106.

are constraints on how long a profession may be delayed. Some come from canon law. Others come from a person's unwillingness to take extra time, from the desire to keep a group together, or from the expectations of the community.

Here are some questions that may help to clarify whether an otherwise suitable person is at the stage of prudently going on to the next level of monastic initiation.

1. *Does the person give evidence of having attained a solid degree of affective or emotional maturity?* It is obviously unwise to profess a person who has not attained adulthood. Equally, it is unrealistic to expect that anyone will ever be fully mature and fully free from occasional pockets of childishness. Since some degree of regression is not uncommon during the years of formation and is implicitly (if unconsciously) demanded by formation structures, one of the clearest signs of a readiness for profession is the revival of full adulthood.[8] Usually this takes place during the years of temporary profession, provided that the person has been encouraged to act out of personal freedom, is not afraid of being seen as he or she is, and is able to be bold, to exercise initiative, and to do things with style. Of course, this may be a very good route to getting

---

8. The following are the signs of emotional maturity as given by psychologist Br. Ronald Fogarty, FMS: The person (1) chooses life rather than misery; (2) has an unobstructed capacity for personal development (self-actualization); (3) has a firm sense of identity; (4) is self-accepting; (5) is not paralyzed by inner conflicts, fears, doubts, scruples, inconsistencies, divisions; (6) is reality-oriented, not reality-avoiding (i.e., has unobstructed cognitive efficacy); (7) accepts responsibility for his or her own life and actions; (8) accepts responsibility for long-range planning and action; (9) has a high tolerance and is emotionally stable in times of stress, frustration, disappointment, anguish, or shock; (10) is able to cope with what is unknown, unplanned, or uncontrollable; (11) manifests a will to understand what is happening without evasion, without blaming others, or without dismissing self too rapidly; and (12) is prepared to regulate the mind's activity, quieting the emotions to permit the reason to be active.

into trouble sometimes. On the other hand, those who are not prepared sometimes to make trouble often don't make much of their lives.

2. *Have the major issues in the person's life been adequately addressed?* The uncovering of these issues and the devising of strategies and tactics to deal with them should have been major concerns during the years of initial formation. This means that a person has, with the help of formators, attained a high level of critical self-awareness, not only at the emotional and psychological level but also spiritually. Formation is possible only in the context of a person's story. Unless that story has been fully told, fully listened to, and fully heard, there can be no confidence that it is the *real* person who is presenting himself or herself for profession. If this storytelling has been well done, it is likely that candidates will know themselves better, having discovered new facets of their experience through the process of sharing it with a formator. A sure sign of this development is that candidates can confront their own inner darkness without undue shame, even as they share these burdens with another. Where there are areas of concealment, be they deliberate or not, be they ever so minor, the confidence to go forward is undermined. To be accepted as one is, fully known, warts and all, is a good guarantee of an authentic vocation.

3. *Is there a high degree of conscious acceptance of all elements of personal history?* Once the whole story has been told in ever-widening circles, the task of warm and realistic self-acceptance remains. Without a complete picture of self, there is a possibility that later on the unprocessed factors—such as degree of intelligence, race, sexuality (including sexual orientation), family background, talents and skills (or their absence), and personal tragedy—will burst forth vigorously and demand attention. It is not prudent to profess an unknown quantity. As growth continues, it is inevitable that all that is now hidden

will burst forth into the light of day. Most of this self-discovery should take place while the person is still in a situation where support and guidance are feasible. After profession, problems often isolate those who experience them from the very people who could help them most.[9]

4. *Is the person able freely to discuss present difficulties and temptations and not only those that are already resolved?* Past failings are relatively easy to admit, especially when we are aware that statistically such lapses are virtually universal. In one sense it is simply confessing our normality. To be open about present struggles and failures is likely to occasion much greater shame and reticence. The fact that we are trying to overcome a particular weakness or vice and are not succeeding is hard to live with. So we tend to split off the aberrant behavior and push it below the threshold of consciousness. To live in the awareness of ongoing moral defects is an indication that the person's conscience is functioning as it should. Such honesty is a prime source of the prized monastic quality of humility. One who has developed the skill of being able to take counsel on personal problems will surely find it easier to weather the inevitable storms that a normal monastic future will bring. Furthermore, a willingness to seek advice should be accompanied by the willingness to act upon it. It is always a good sign when a candidate is prepared to go beyond some personal limitation or failure and, in trustful obedience to a formator or superior, to abandon some cherished delusion or to move into a field of activity for which they feel no attraction or aptitude.

5. *Has the person passed through several significant crises in the years of formation?* What have been the means used during these difficult times? Some tend to take a vacation from monastic

---

9. Vincent and George Bilotta have devised a process of structured autobiography that gives the person the chance to explore every facet of their personal history. This is available from Formation Consultation Services, Inc.

conversatio when the going gets tough; others realize that in times of struggle greater fidelity to the monastic means will more likely lead to the resolution of difficulties than letting them lapse. Crises are generally means of breaking apart the rudimentary levels of integration achieved at various levels in the course of a lifetime. It may seem like disaster, but in fact it is an opportunity for great growth when the person gathers together the pieces and constructs a new entity that better accords with the challenges of the higher state into which (unbeknownst to themselves) they are already entering. One who has never experienced such a crisis is living in a state of stagnation. If such crises have not happened yet, then this means that they will happen in the future.

6. *Does the person indicate a sense of being at home in the community by an easy acceptance of community rituals and symbols?* Sometimes candidates are careful to conform in all substantive matters during the period of probation, concealing from others any resentment they may feel at the encroachment on their personal liberty. After final profession such restraint is quickly shed, and a certain irregularity may begin to be noticed, particularly in the area of punctuality and attendance at community exercises. Being aware of nonconformity in minor matters before profession may serve as an indicator of potential major aberration afterward. Some examples of community symbols or usages may include the accepted use of the habit, the observance of seniority, carefulness in liturgical rituals such as bows, the use of "in-language," and the like. A chronic tendency to singularity, to doing everything in a self-chosen manner, often indicates a reluctance to be and to be seen as one of the community and a desire to stand out from the rest and be noticed. Where this is manifest, it is worth exploring.

7. *Is there a subjective sense that monastic life is the "one way" to salvation? Do vocation and salvation coincide?* One manifestation of this is a relative lack of interest in alternative forms of Chris-

tian discipleship. A certain eagerness about monastic spirituality is a good sign and, for example, among Cistercians, a real sense of affinity with the classical expressions of the Cistercian spirit. On the other hand, it would seem wiser to defer the profession of those whose *primary* spirituality is drawn from other sources, such as Marian apparitions, Pentecostalism, yoga or zen, and certain types of devotionalism, until such time as there is evidence that the candidate's life is solidly grounded on basic monastic principles. The problem is not so much the content that is drawn from other spiritualities as the obstinacy that makes some people choose a singular path while remaining somewhat indifferent to the common course of the community. A strongly apophatic spirituality does not readily provide incentives for a lifelong commitment to community, liturgy, and creative work, even though it may be a providential means of survival at a time when one or more of these areas go sour. Likewise, a passion for social justice is likely to be frustrated by the restraints of monastic enclosure and to give rise to mere feelings that have no outflow in actions. Fifty years ago, most monastic vocations brought with them an eclectic mix of spiritualities, symbolized by devotions associated with particular saints: Thérèse of Lisieux (the "little way"), Margaret Mary (Sacred Heart), Grignion de Montfort ("true devotion" to Mary), the Carmelite mystics if they were so inclined, and many more. In those days it was possible to muddle through on such a diet, since monasticism was often understood simply as observance, and whatever helped at a practical level was found acceptable. Today, when commitment is much wobblier, good observance by itself is not a sufficient sign: it needs to be complemented by monastic beliefs and values that are deep enough to enable the person to adapt to both the internal and the external change that the future living of monastic *conversatio* will demand.

8. *Does the person approach profession without an implicit career path?* In the case of monks, this means without the presumption

that they will be called to priesthood quickly. For all, profession needs to be made on the understanding that others will decide how best to make use of their talents. This will happen not according to the person's own assessment but in the context of the community's needs and opportunities and in the spirit of Saint Benedict's chapter 57, "On the Artisans in the Monastery." In other words, possibilities for employment and further training or studies will be assessed according to their potential contribution to the person's monastic perseverance and also according to possible benefits for the community. If they are likely to undermine a vocation, they will be sacrificed to the greater good. Just as negative, in terms of placing conditions on self-giving, is a species of trade-union minimalism, defining demarcation limits on what tasks may be assigned and insisting on guaranteed rights and privileges.

9. *Is the person sufficiently autonomous to navigate the vicissitudes of community life, spiritual transitions, and temptations without the close attention routinely provided by formators?* When a person passes out of the immediate care of formators, many taken-for-granted supports are lost. The usual expectation is that the newly professed will be able to stand on their own feet. Of course, they are not totally alone; superiors and others continue to provide pastoral care, at least theoretically. What has to be assessed is the candidates' capacity not only for survival but also for continued growth through the acceptance of unexpected challenges, especially those occasioned by a greater degree of personal freedom. For most this will involve continuing attention to the journey of self-knowledge and will involve the choice of a spiritual director, mentor, or supervisor whom they will allow to help them in the process.

*   *   *

Not all these questions will be relevant to all, nor will they all be unequivocally answered with an affirmative response. Formators, superiors, and others involved in the decision-making process are not infallible. Sometimes, despite diligent investigation, they will not have access to all the data. Sometimes they will choose to give a candidate the benefit of the doubt, hoping for the best. Sometimes, swayed by affection, the community's needs, or inattention, they will make a misjudgment. Sometimes it becomes clear only after several years of trying that a person has no monastic vocation and that it would be cruel and inhuman to insist that they remain. As with all practical judgments, we can do no more than our reasonable best, trusting in the providence of God that sometimes allows mistakes to be made in the furtherance of a loftier goal. It is always something of a consolation to hear, years afterward, that someone who has left monastic life has come to believe that their years in the monastery were not wasted. But it is obviously in our own best interests that we try to ensure that there is a good likelihood that those we admit to profession will persevere; otherwise, we will pay the price, in more senses than one.

Chapter Eleven

NEVER LOSE HEART

After listing all the good works in which monks ought to engage, Saint Benedict adds the recommendation, "Never lose hope in God's mercy" (RB 4.74). Now that we have elaborated an equally long catalogue of things to consider in the matter of initial monastic formation, a similar message needs to be delivered. To all monastic formators I say: *Do not allow yourselves to become discouraged*. The pastoral care of newcomers to the monastery is a "hard and difficult thing" (RB 2.31). It has its failures and disappointments, but ultimately it is a great contribution to the quality of monastic life in the present and for the future. And, in more sanguine moods, it can be a source of quiet gratification to formators when they see those in their care making profession or, in later years, cheerfully living the life to which they were formed.

I have had the privilege of meeting and working with a large number of monastic formators over the past decades, and it has been my impression that although these men and women are persons of high caliber and are dedicated to monastic life and to their work as formators, mostly they feel insecure in their work and powerless to accomplish much good. On the one hand, there never is an exact recipe for helping the particular people in their care at a particular time; on the other, there is always an element of insecurity because they have no guarantee that a sudden revelation of new aspects of personality or history is not just around the corner.

Many formators have passed through a period in which they had to work with someone with whom they experienced serious difficulty despite their best efforts. While it is true that the cause of the difficulty is commonly found in both parties, the relative share is not always equal. Difficult people exist.[1] Formators have enough to do without blaming themselves for failing to maintain a harmonious and productive relationship with persons who (consciously or not) do everything in their power to subvert their efforts. I am sometimes consoled by what canon law has to say: "Novices, conscious of their own responsibility, are to cooperate actively with the director of novices" (can. 652.2, CIC). The maintenance of a good relationship does not depend totally on the formator.

Formators are quickly confronted with two major philosophical questions: the phenomenon of free will and the mystery of sin. It may be some consolation to remember that even the best of formators could not prevent Judas from his act of betrayal. We too will sometimes find ourselves impotent to dissuade someone from a choice that is not life-giving, in minor matters as well as at the major junctures of life. There is no remedy that can be applied externally for the condition that the Bible names "hardness of heart." This is not necessarily manifested by a harsh or aggressive manner. It can just as easily show itself by a blithe obstinacy, pleasant and smiling, complacent and at peace. A hard heart does not mind listening to contrary arguments because there is no way these can penetrate to its inner sanctum. It listens and, without becoming contentious, replies untruthfully, politely declines any assent, or simply ignores whatever has been said. Sometimes, when a person is on the point of leaving, the semblance of discernment is permitted, but, interiorly, a decision has already been made. The point of no return has been passed. When others make up their minds,

---

1. See Robert M. Bramson, *Coping with Difficult People* (Melbourne: The Business Library, 1981); John Clarke, *Working with Monsters: How to Identify and Protect Yourself from the Workplace Sociopath* (Milsons Point: Random House, 2005); Robert Sutton, *The No Asshole Rule: Building a Civilised Workplace and Surviving One That Isn't* (London: Sphere, 2007); Douglas Stone, Bruce Patton, Sheila Heen, *Difficult Conversations: How to Discuss What Matters Most* (London: Penguin Books, 2000).

the most we can achieve is some measure of damage control. No reasoned argument of ours can change the outcome. We do not have to believe that such decisions are made lightly or in bad faith, but there is no disputing the possibility that sincere choices can lead to unhappy outcomes. The fact is that often we are profoundly ignorant of all the forces that have inclined a person to make a particular choice, as they themselves are also sometimes unaware.

Occasionally, one may encounter strong resistance to grace, whether it takes the form of a deliberate choice for what is death dealing or, more commonly, of a refusal to move forward in an unfamiliar direction. This also is where formators experience their own limits. If grace cannot achieve a positive result, there is little chance that we will succeed.

When those in our care decide to discontinue the monastic journey, we are often disappointed. It is hard to avoid falling captive to the notion that the more persons we graduate, the more successful we are as formators. From there it is but a short step to linking our sense of self-worth to the number of people we hand over to the next stage of their monastic career. The fact that not all who enter will persevere is known in the abstract, but it is still hard when they pack their bags and leave. Sometimes, it is true, we are relieved; there are occasions when we are convinced that, though regrettable, this is the right decision. Every departure, however, is a loss to the community and a personal loss for us. The person whom we had come to know and appreciate will be missed, and our lives are the poorer for it. We have to remind ourselves often that part of our duty during the time of probation is to ensure that those who do not have a monastic vocation find their way out of the monastery. Even in these cases there is sadness. There is also an element of frustration, in the sense that we may have spent many hours in being present to the person, listening to them, and trying to help, with only an apparently inconclusive result.

The situation is not helped when those who do not know the full story allow their disappointment to be translated into blame, with the formator being an obvious target for recrimination. It is said that these candidates should never have been accepted in the first place, that they should have been sent away long ago, that they should have been given a different formation, or that they should (in ways not specified) have been prevented from leaving. Sometimes all of the above are alleged. Since the real reasons behind a particular departure (as distinct from the person's own press releases) are often confidential, the formator can do no other than say nothing.

In all these situations we are brought back to the simple notion that formation is ultimately God's work, from the first intimations of a calling all the way through to final perseverance. Our involvement in the process is secondary at the most. We do our best, and sometimes the results seem to correspond with what we were trying to do. But this is probably a happy coincidence since God does not work according to any blueprint or schedule of ours. Equally, God rarely works except through human agents, and if anything good happens during the years of formation, it is probably because community members and formators have been faithful in living their vocation and doing whatever the situation required. Nevertheless, it is extremely difficult to establish direct causality, either to praise or to blame. I find it hard to believe, however, that good and sensible people generously doing their best can possibly bring about anything that is more bad than good.

Pastoral care of others is a great way to discover one's own limits and is an effective means of teaching us to rely on prayer not only as a source of guidance, energy, and resilience but also as a means of coping with the revelations about ourselves that such work carries with it. The best example of this is the *Pastoral Prayer* of Saint Aelred of Rievaulx. Reflection on this text will yield much profit for many formators and superiors. To be called to act as a formator is to be called to live a more intense spiritual life; this is the only way to survive. The alternatives are disengagement, burnout, or disenchantment.

I know from speaking with other formators that their work is sometimes a source of great suffering. Uncertainties, anxieties, regrets, and all kinds of negative feelings can cast a shadow over their lives and make their everyday burdens even harder to bear. As a result, there is a fairly constant call to practice the kind of redemptive patience about which Saint Benedict speaks at the end of the Rule's Prologue. Perhaps there is a deeper element in their relationship with those in their care than merely instruction, support, and advice. If it is by the Cross that we are saved, it is also by the Cross that, in some mysterious way, we mediate salvation to others. When Saint Benedict says that formators should be "skilled in winning souls" (RB 58.6), it may be that he is also implying a spiritual and redemptive component of that office: the willingness on the part of formators to bear the burdens of others in their hearts and in their prayer.

I would hope that the underlying message of this book is to encourage formators to keep casting their bread upon the waters. It is a privilege to serve in this role, and despite its labors it provides the possibility of some important collateral benefits. Among these I would mention especially an enhanced self-knowledge, a better understanding of the inner face of monastic experience, and the occasional opportunity to witness the transfiguration that occurs when God's love is fully accepted.

Perhaps the note on which to conclude is an observation made by Fr. Raymond P. Carey, a behavioral psychologist with much experience in the areas of vocational assessment and formation: "In the end, the more closely I have worked with ministers of formation and vocation, the more convinced I am that, if there is any merit to our Church's canonization process, it may well be for those who serve in those ministries."[2]

---

2. Raymond P. Carey, "Combining the Roles of Vocation and Formation Director Creates an Ethical Minefield," *VocNet* 2.1 (Spring 1998) 12.

BIBLIOGRAPHY

Allen, John L. Jr. *The Future Church: How Ten Trends Are Revolutionizing the Catholic Church.* New York: Doubleday, 2009.
Arbuckle, Gerald A. *Dealing with Bullies: A Gospel Response to the Social Disease of Adult Bullying.* Strathfield: St Pauls, 2003.
———. "Multiculturalism, Internationality and Religious Life." *Review for Religious* 54, no. 3 (May–June 1995): 326–38.
———. "Planning the Novitiate Process: Reflections of an Anthropologist." *Review for Religious* 43, no. 4 (July–August 1984): 532–46.
Baker, Russell. "Talking It Up." *The New York Review of Books* 53, no. 8 (11 May 2006): 4–5.
Baron-Cohen, Simon. *Autism and Asperger Syndrome.* Oxford: Oxford University Press, 2008.
———. *The Essential Difference: The Truth about the Male and Female Brain.* New York: Basic Books, 2003.
Bell, Gail. "The Worried Well: The Depression Epidemic and the Medicalisation of Our Sorrows." *Quarterly Essay* 18 (2005): 1–74.
Bendyna, Mary. "Address to LCWR on Vocations to Religious Life Study." *Origins* 39, no. 12 (27 August 2009): 200–5.
Bloom, Allan. "The Study of Texts." in *Giants and Dwarfs: Essays 1960–1990,* 295–314. New York: Simon and Schuster, 1990.
Bramson, Robert M. *Coping with Difficult People.* Melbourne: The Business Library, 1981.
Brown, Alan. *Valuing Skills: Recognition of Prior Learning.* North Melbourne: The Victorian Education Foundation, 1992.
Carey, Raymond P. "Combining the Roles of Vocation and Formation Director Creates an Ethical Minefield." *VocNet* 2, no. 1 (Spring 1998): 11–12.
———. "Pedophilia and Ephebophilia: Vocational Assessment Helps for Identifying 'At-Risk' Candidates." *VocNet* 5, no. 3 (Winter 2002): 4–5.
Carr, Nicholas. *The Shallows: What the Internet Is Doing to Our Brains.* New York: W. W. Norton & Company, 2010.

Casey, Michael. "The Book of Experience: The Western Monastic Art of *Lectio Divina*." *Eye of the Heart* 2 (2008): 5–32.
———. "The Deconstruction of Prayer." *Tjurunga* 51 (1996): 91–102.
———. "Diagnosis and Discernment: *Ut Sapiens Medicus*." *Tjurunga* 74 (2008): 91–96.
———. "'Emotionally Hollow, Esthetically Meaningless and Spiritually Empty': An Inquiry into Theological Discourse." *Colloquium* 14, no. 1 (1981): 54–61.
———. "The Formative Influence of the Benedictine Community." *Tjurunga* 14 (1977): 7–26.
———. "Marketing Monastic Tradition within Monasteries." *Tjurunga* 60 (2001): 27–52; reprinted in *An Unexciting Life: Reflections on Benedictine Spirituality* (Petersham, MA: St. Bede's Publications, 2005) 407–43.
———. "Modelling: A Challenge for Formators." *Tjurunga* 75 (2008): 18–30.
———. "Models of Monastic Formation." *Tjurunga* 45 (1993): 3–31; reprinted in *An Unexciting Life*, 361–405.
———. "The Rule of Saint Benedict and Inculturation: A Formation Perspective." *Tjurunga* 62 (2002): 15–46; reprinted in *An Unexciting Life*, 449–90.
———. "Sacramentality and Monastic Consecration." *Word and Spirit* 18 (1998): 27–48; reprinted in *An Unexciting Life*, 263–85.
———. *Strangers to the City: Reflections on the Beliefs and Values of the Rule of Saint Benedict*. Brewster: Paraclete Press, 2005.
Center for Applied Research in the Apostolate (CARA). "CARA Report on Recent Vocations to Religious Life in the U.S." *Origins* 39, no.12 (22 August 2009): 193–200.
Chaminade, Benjamin. "Fidélisation versus retention." (8 June 2003). www.focusrh.com/article.php3?id_article=107.
Clarke, John. *Working with Monsters: How to Identify and Protect Yourself from the Workplace Sociopath*. Milsons Point: Random House, 2005.
Cleary, Guire, ssf. "Challenges for Communities' New Members." *Review for Religious* 65, no. 1 (2006): 30–42.
Covey, Stephen M. R., with Rebecca R. Merrill. *The Speed of Trust: The One Thing That Changes Everything*. New York: Free Press, 2006.
Covey, Stephen R. *The Seven Habits of Highly Effective People*. Melbourne: The Business Library, 1990.

———. *The 8th Habit: From Effectiveness to Greatness.* New York: Free Press, 2005.

Crews, Frederick. "Out, Damned Blot!" *The New York Review of Books* 51, no. 12 (15 July 2004): 22–25.

Davies, Robertson, *The Rebel Angels.* Harmondsworth: Penguin Books, 1981.

Deal, Jennifer. *Retiring the Generation Gap: How Employees Young and Old Can Find Common Ground.* San Francisco: Jossey-Bass, 2007.

Dobbs, David. "Beautiful Brains." *National Geographic* 220, no. 4 (October 2011): 36–59.

Dumont, Charles. "St Aelred: The Balanced Life of the Monk." *Monastic Studies* 1 (1963): 25–38.

Dulles, Avery. *Models of Revelation.* Garden City: Doubleday, 1983.

———. *Models of the Church.* Garden City: Doubleday, 1974.

Ekman, Paul. *Telling Lies: Clues to Deceit in the Marketplace, Politics and Marriage.* New ed. New York: W. W. Norton & Company, 2009.

Fangman, Esther, OSB. "Listening Turns the Soul to God." *Benedictines* 63, no. 2 (Fall–Winter 2010): 6–16.

Fleming, David L. "Individualism in Community Life." *Human Development* 21, no. 3 (Fall 2000): 5–12.

Flynn, Stephen E. "America the Resilient: Defying Terrorism and Mitigating Natural Disasters." *Foreign Affairs* 87, no. 2 (2008): 2–8.

Gadamer, Hans-Georg. *Truth and Method.* London: Sheed and Ward, 1965.

Gallagher, John, "Individualism and Religious Life." *Review for Religious* 54, no. 4 (1995): 585–88.

Glock, Charles Y., Benjamin B. Ringer, and Earl R. Babbie. *To Comfort and to Challenge: A Dilemma of the Contemporary Church.* Berkeley: University of California Press, 1967.

Goldberg, Elkhonon. *The Wisdom Paradox: How Your Mind Can Grow Stronger as Your Brain Grows Older.* New York: Gotham Books, 2005.

Goleman, Daniel. *Emotional Intelligence: Why It Can Matter More than IQ.* London: Bloomsbury, 1996.

———. *Social Intelligence: The New Science of Human Relationships.* London: Hutchinson, 2006.

Hamilton, Andrew, SJ. "Forty Years Away." *Eureka Street* 12.8 (October 2002): 36–37.

Hanby, Michael. "The Culture of Death, the Ontology of Boredom, and the Resistance of Joy." *Communio* 31, no. 2 (Summer 2004): 184–85.

Jeremias, Joachim. *New Testament Theology, Part One: The Proclamation of Jesus*. London: SCM Press, 1971.

Keenan, James. "HIV Testing of Seminary and Religious-Order Candidates." *Review for Religious* 55, no. 3 (May–June 1996): 297–314.

Leavey, Matthew, John Klassen, Paul Schwietz, Robin Pierzina, and Robert Pierson. "Qualities and Skills for Monastic Life: One Approach." *Benedictines* 54, no. 1 (2001): 6–13.

Lerner, Ulrich L. *Enlightened Monks: The German Benedictines, 1740–1803*. Oxford: Oxford University Press, 2011.

Levinson, Daniel J. *The Seasons of a Man's Life*. New York: Ballantine Books, 1978.

Louf, André, *Grace Can Do More: Spiritual Accompaniment and Spiritual Growth*. Kalamazoo, MI: Cistercian Publications, 2002.

Mackay, Hugh, *Social Disengagement: A Breeding Ground for Fundamentalism*. Sixth Annual Manning Clark Lecture (3 March 2005).

May, Gerald G. *Addiction and Grace: Love and Spirituality in the Healing of Addictions*. San Francisco: HarperSanFrancisco, 1991.

McNamara, Kevin E. "Psychological Screening for Religious Life." *Review for Religious* 54, no. 4 (July–August 1995): 589–93.

Merton, Thomas. *The Climate of Monastic Prayer*. Spencer, MA: Cistercian Publications, 1970.

———. "Prayer, Tradition, and Experience." In *Thomas Merton in Alaska: The Alaskan Conferences, Journals, and Letters*, 115–27. New York: New Directions, 1989.

Michaud, Christophe. "The Power of Strength and the Power of Weakness." *Tjurunga* 58 (2000): 71–88.

Mishima, Yukio. *Spring Snow*. Tokyo: Charles E. Tuttle Company, 1972.

Nussbaum, Martha C. *Hiding from Humanity: Disgust, Shame and the Law*. Princeton, NJ: Princeton University Press, 2004.

Nutting, Geoffrey. *On Becoming More Open to Others in God: Asperger Syndrome and the Enneagram*. DMin thesis, Melbourne College of Divinity, 2009.

Olivera, Bernardo. "Our Young and Not So Young Monks and Nuns." Conference given at the OCSO General Chapters, September 2002.

Palmer, Parker J. *The Courage to Teach: Exploring the Inner Landscape of a Teacher's Life*. San Francisco: Jossey-Bass, 1998.

———. *Let Your Life Speak: Listening for the Voice of Vocation*. San Francisco: Jossey-Bass, 2000.

Pembroke, Neil. *The Art of Listening: Dialogue, Shame and Pastoral Care*. Edinburgh: T&T Clark, 2002.

Peter, Simon, SJ. "Alcoholism and Jesuit Life: An Individual and Community Illness." *Studies in the Spirituality of Jesuits* 13, no.1 (January 1981): 1–66.

Postman, Neil. *Amusing Ourselves to Death: Public Discourse in the Age of Show Business*. New York: Penguin Books, 2005.

Putnam, Robert D. *Bowling Alone: The Collapse and Revival of American Community*. New York: Simon & Schuster, 2001.

Radcliffe, Timothy. *Sing a New Song: The Christian Vocation*. Dublin: Dominican Publications, 2000.

Rahner, Hugo. *Man at Play; or, Did You Ever Practise Eutrapelia?* Translated by Brian Battershaw and Edward Quinn. London: Burns & Oates, 1965.

Rahner, Karl. "The Spirituality of the Church of the Future." In *Theological Investigations*, vol. 20, *Concern for the Church*, 148–49. Translated by Edward Quinn. London: Darton, Longman & Todd, 1981.

Rancé, Armand-Jean de. *La Régle de saint Benoist nouvellement traduite et éxpliquée selon son veritable esprit*. Paris: François Muguet and George & Louis Josse, 1689.

Ridley, Matt. *Nature via Nurture: Genes, Experience and What Makes Us Human*. London: Fourth Estate, 2003.

Rosenberg, Marshall B. *Nonviolent Communication: A Language of Life*. Encinita, CA: PuddleDancer Press, 2003.

Rulla, Luigi M., Franco Imoda, and Joyce Ridick. *Psychological Structure and Vocation: A Study of the Motivations for Entering and Leaving the Religious Life*. Dublin: Villa Books, 1979.

Sammon, Seán. "Rekindling the Fire!" at www.champagnat.org/shared/Scritti_Sean/SeanCarlaChama_EN.pdf.

———. "Renewal of Religious Life in the US." *Origins* 40, no. 19 (14 October 2010): 289–96.

Sipe, A. W. Richard. *Celibacy: A Way of Loving, Living, and Serving*. Alexandria, NSW: E. J. Dwyer, 1996.

Stewart, Jenny. "In Praise of Teaching." *Eureka Street* 16.3 (May–June 2006): 36–37.

Steyn, Mark. "The Entertainment State." *The New Criterion* 17, no. 1 (September 1998): 24–29.

Stone, Douglas, Bruce Patton, and Sheila Heen. *Difficult Conversations: How to Discuss What Matters Most*. London: Penguin Books, 2000.

Sutera, Judith, OSB. "Vocations on a New Frontier." *Benedictines* 54, no. 1 (Spring–Summer 2001): 14–21.

Sutton, Robert. *The No Asshole Rule: Building a Civilised Workplace and Surviving One That Isn't.* London: Sphere, 2007.

Vaughan, Diane. *Uncoupling: How and Why Relationships Fall Apart.* London: Methuen, 1987.

Vogüé, Adalbert de. *Community and Abbot in the Rule of Saint Benedict.* Kalamazoo, MI: Cistercian Publications, 1988.

Waddell, Chrysogonus. *Narrative and Legislative Texts from Early Cîteaux.* Cîteaux: Commentarii Cistercienses, 1999.

Wilson, Katherine. "The Rhythm of Engagement." *Overland* 201 (Summer 2010): 14.

Zavala, Gabino. "Social Media: Friend or Foe, Google or Hornswoggle?" *Origins* 40, no. 25 (25 November 2010): 392–94.